Friends for the Journey

Friends for the Journey

*Two extraordinary women celebrate
friendships made and sustained
through the seasons of life*

Madeleine L'Engle
AND Luci Shaw

SERVANT PUBLICATIONS
ANN ARBOR, MICHIGAN

Vine Books is an imprint of Servant Publications especially designed to serve evangelical Christians.

The following poems that appear in this book are used by permission of their publisher. "Madeleine's Candlesticks" by Luci Shaw. Used by permission of *Radix* magazine, vol. 23, No.4, 1995. "Finding Myself," "Spring: St. Martin's Chapel," and "Eating the Whole Egg" from *Writing the River*, © 1994 by Luci Shaw. Used by permission of NavPress Publishing Group. For copies call 1-800-366-7788.

"Common Ground," "Questions 1985," "The Risk of Love," "The Partaking," "Salutation," "Gifts for My Girl," "Prothalamion," "Judas, Peter," "Spice," "The Separation," and "At the Church of the Savior, Washington, D.C." are from *Polishing the Petoskey Stone*, © 1990 by Luci Shaw. Used by permission of Harold Shaw Publishers, 388 Gundersen Drive, Wheaton, Illinois 60189.

"Possess Your Soul in Patience" by Luci Shaw, originally published in the Summer 1996 Issue of *Mars Hill Review* (1-800-990-MARS). Used by permission of *Mars Hill Review*.

"A Time of Peril," "God's Beast," "Epiphany," "To a Long Loved Love," "Lovers Apart" from *The Weather of the Heart* by Madeleine L'Engle, © 1978 by Crosswicks. Used by permission of Harold Shaw Publishers, 388 Gundersen Drive, Wheaton, Illinois 60189.

Published by Servant Publications
P.O. Box 8617
Ann Arbor, Michigan 48107

Published in association with the literary agency of Alive Communications, 1465 Kelly Johnson Blvd., Suite #320, Colorado Springs, CO 80920.

Cover design: PAZ Design Group, Salem, Oregon
Cover photo: Barbara Braver

    98 99 00 01   10 9 8 7 6 5 4 3 2

Printed in the United States of America
ISBN 0-89283-986-4

LIBRARY OF CONGRESS CATALOGING-IN-PUBLICATION DATA

L'Engle, Madeleine.
Friends for the journey / Madeleine L'Engle and Luci Shaw.
    p.   cm.
ISBN 0-89283-986-4
1. L'Engle, Madeleine—Friends and associates.   2. Women authors, American—20th century—Biography.   I. Shaw, Luci.   II. Title.
PS3523.E55Z465   1997
813'.54—dc21   97-2356
[B]   CIP

To Bara, our editor
and the third person in our trinity of friendship

Contents

Preface

We're twenty-five years into knowing each other. So, when we were asked if we would consider collaborating on a book on friendship, we immediately and instinctively said, *Yes!* because we felt that the idea of deep, true friendship is being diminished in favor of an undifferentiated sea of "relationships," and that the need for friendship should be seen anew, and revived, and redeemed.

This book itself will tell many of our reasons for writing. Perhaps one of the most significant is that, close and warm as it is, ours has never been an exclusive friendship. It is based on *Hesed,* the evocative Hebrew word that means loving-kindness, reaching-out compassion, grace. *Hesed* is a reflection, an outgrowth in our lives, of the mercy and compassion of the God we both worship, whose love is inclusive rather than exclusive.

Hesed speaks not only of a disposition; it is borne out in actions. And it is out of this *Hesed* heart-attitude that the action of this book is being offered to you.

We—Madeleine and Luci—have a friendship that is far from perfect; our motives are often muddled, muddied, and mixed. Our theology is evolving. That is where God comes in. God has challenged, encouraged, and warmed us through the gift of each other, a gift which must not reach a dead end in us.

In fact, it has not. In our neurotic and fragmented culture, in which many values are being abandoned and not replaced, and which badly needs healing, we offer our reflections as a way of honoring friendship.

What we continue to learn of love and kinship is being enriched by what we gain from, and what we give to many other friends, chiefly, in the case of the present volume, Barbara Braver, our friend and editor.

We've received the experience of each other as a gift. Here's to friendship! And here—the gift of friendship given to you—holy, happy, tough, tender, wild, wacky, a sacrifice and a sacrament.

Luci Shaw and Madeleine L'Engle
Crosswicks Cottage
August, 1996

A Table for Two:

Our own stories

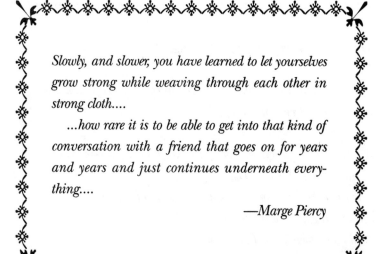

Slowly, and slower, you have learned to let yourselves grow strong while weaving through each other in strong cloth....

...how rare it is to be able to get into that kind of conversation with a friend that goes on for years and years and just continues underneath everything....

—Marge Piercy

A time of peril.
A crash and scream of metal, glass
A time of near death, death's wings so close the cold wind brushed my
face.
Then a slow awakening, light hurting, pain stabbing
Loneliness.
A hospital bed. I.C.U. San Diego. A continent away from home.
Midsummer. Everyone away.
Loneliness.
A strange loud jangling. I jump in fear. What? Oh—the phone.
Hard to reach. Hurts. "Hello?"
It is Luci. Home from abroad. Home in San Francisco.
"Madeleine, do you want me to come?"
And then, even before I have time
to give the mandatory, polite, negative answer
"Madeleine, I'm coming."
Friendship.
Yes. Oh yes.

Madeleine

This is a real, deep, long friendship, Luci's and mine, built up over a quarter of a century. Built up over shared joys and griefs. The deaths, one following upon the other, of our husbands, in one year. The growing of our trust in God's love. Sharing our children's joys and sorrows. Cooking. Lighting candles. Sitting around the table. Talking about the events of the day, in our own lives, in a world full of hope and wonder, grief and tragedy.

Today I am happy because Luci is coming. Our friendship started when we first met at Wheaton College. I was there as part of a conference on art and faith, and Luci had come to participate. Our friendship began quickly because I loved the book of poetry she gave me, *Listen to the Green*, and she loved my book, *A Circle of Quiet*. There we were, spread out on the page for each other. Immediately we knew that we shared much: in our struggle to live what once upon a time was called "a godly life"; in our attitude about our writing—which we both saw as vocation rather than career; in our love for our families and our feelings about marriage.

Our backgrounds are superficially so different that there was much each of us had to learn to understand. Luci grew up on several continents in the evangelical world of the Plymouth Brethren. I grew up in metropolitan New York and Europe in an Episcopal family. We both believe in a God of love, yet there have been radical and unexpected differences. We both believed in the miracle of the cross and resurrection, yet Luci believes (like most good Evangelicals) that Jesus had to die on the cross in order for God to forgive us. I believe (like most Episcopalians) that God was on the cross, in Jesus, because of love, not anger, love. Amazingly, this radical difference in interpretation has been a source of conversation, learning, and prayer, rather than acrimony.

We pray together. We prayed our way into friendship. We prayed in anguish, mostly on the phone, as first Luci's husband, then mine, sickened with cancer and died. Neither of us believed that an angry God had deliberately afflicted these two good men; that is not the nature of love. We knew that God could come into the tragedies we did not understand, that God cared about us and what was happening. We were willing to share our hopes and fears, to pick up the phone simply because we needed to hear the other's voice.

Even when we cried together, Luci and I have always been ready to break into laughter at the next moment. We helped each other move back into life after our husbands' deaths. We've rescued each other over and over again, not always dramatically, as when Luci came to me in San Diego, but sometimes simply by not being shocked at the words or emotions of the other.

Working together on a book about friendship has been not only an amazing challenge but a delight. We have spent time thinking and talking together about the need to celebrate and honor friendship in a culture of superficial relationships. We have rejoiced in each other in a new way. We have rejoiced in our ability to be vulnerable with one another, and our opportunity to be vulnerable as we share in these pages our lives, our thoughts, and our sense of the grace and glory *and absolute necessity* of friendship.

The Table as Icon

Luci

How often Madeleine and I have sat at table together. The dining room table—where I used to live in West Chicago, or at my little house in Bellingham, or Madeleine's apartment in New York, or at Crosswicks Cottage—has been the setting for so many meals by candlelight, with linen and silver and flowers. As we sat there, either the two of us alone, or with other friends of the heart, always we were glad for such occasions of joy and celebration.

Perhaps the table which is for me the truest icon of our friendship is Madeleine's dining room table in New York City, worn to a mellow beauty that borrows not only from the candle flames and flowers but from the faces of all the friends who have gathered to partake of every meal there, served with grace and generosity (Madeleine is a superb cook), eaten with gratitude and gusto.

That table has also had another function. Often, during a day of editorial or proofreading work together, it has served as our editorial desk, piled with books and papers, decorated with rubber bands and paper clips. Even the cats are part of the creative clutter. Their favorite resting places are invariably the manuscripts we are working on *right now*. And if they're not napping on our brilliant ideas they're rolling pencils along the surface, tapping them with delicately curled paws. Tatiana, the all-white princess, reclines at one end in regal splendor. Kelly and Terrible, the black and white duo, are more aggressive, arching their backs under our chins and curling their tails seductively around our necks, distracting us until we pick them up bodily from the table and lower them to the floor, firmly informing them that *that* is their place. Then, before dinner we tidy up, set the table, and light the candles. We hold hands, singing the blessing before we begin to eat.

We both remember the first time we met for a meal, at my house near Wheaton, shortly after we met at Wheaton College. The occasion was a Language and Literature conference, and we were both participants. The conversation we began there has lasted a quarter of a century, and we both hope we have a similar span of time ahead of us. Our contact was never superficial; it started out, as it has continued, with God talk and book talk, the elements of the kind of friendship we both find the most satisfying. I gave Madeleine a copy of *Listen to the Green,* my first book of poems. She responded with *A Circle of Quiet,* and as I read it later I remember thinking—*How much we have in common! We both love to play Bach, we both need the tranquillity of green space in woods, by streams, we both burn the peas when our minds are on loftier matters.*

In correspondence I learned that Madeleine's book of poetry, *Lines Scribbled on an Envelope,* had just gone out of print, and publisher that I was, I asked her if she'd like us to reprint it, along with some of her more recent poems. When she responded with enthusiasm, our author/editor relationship had begun! Since then we have worked together on eight more of her books, starting with *Walking on Water,* her reflections on faith and art, which has continued to be a best seller in the world that we both inhabit, where faith and art are both vital. The universe is itself a work of art, with God as the first Artist, the first Poet, and we both acknowledge our calling by this Maker to be co-creators, with God, with each other.

But the relationship soon transcended the professional. I had had a classically Evangelical upbringing, Madeleine comes from an equally classical Episcopalian background. Our instruction and training in the Christian faith have been dramatically different. As we have both questioned, even doubted, and disagreed—without acrimony though often with vigor—and reached together for deeper and truer understandings of God's ways with us, we have met in the middle, and nudged each other to continue to grow.

When my innate sacramentalism moved me, with my husband Harold, to enter the Episcopal church, and Madeleine and I began to share the holy food and drink at the Lord's table, we found that kneeling together at the altar was a profound and marvelous way of affirming love and friendship with each other, and with our God.

Together we have shared the stresses and recompenses of parenthood; the drawn-out deaths by cancer of both our husbands, Harold and Hugh, in the same year; the rocky path of bereavement and grief which raised in both of us existential questions about the meaning of life itself, and of our lives. These uncertainties have always led us to prayer, and prayer together, touching God, is, as Ecclesiastes tells us, a three-fold cord which is not quickly broken, a cord which thickens and strengthens with the years.

As we have passed together through both tragedy and triumph, through weakness and failure, we affirm that our friendship has not only been significant but that it has, on occasion, quite literally saved us in times of desperate need.

This has required a degree of honesty with each other, which is the basis of true intimacy in a world where intimacy is often traded for superficiality.

Last year I wrote in my journal,

On the eve of departure from New York I just had time for my now customary polishing of Madeleine's candlesticks. Suddenly I realize I'm dealing with more than "just" candlesticks; I'm coming to think of it as "polishing Madeleine." Then I notice something I've missed before, her name (misspelled "Madeline") inscribed, faint but dark, on the base of two of the four silver candle-holders, and the idea of the polishing of a friend, and a friendship, turns even truer. It's a variation on the theme of the biblical proverb: "As iron sharpens iron, so the heart of friend with friend."

Though we may need a kind of corrective sharpening from each other from time to time, polishing is a gentler art. As writers, critics, editors, wordsmiths, we polish each other's phrases and ideas. Yesterday I read Madeleine my new poem "Eucalyptus." After I'd fallen silent at the end of the poem, she said, without pre-amble, "Take off the last three lines." And she was absolutely right. Those lines were redundant, part of the scaffolding of the poem which needed to be peeled away to reveal the poem's central struc-ture and integrity. So our roles of writer and editor reverse—often, easily, effortlessly. And we continue to luster each other to a shine in the joy of a friendship blessed by God.

Beyond that, beyond the written or spoken work we produce are our very selves, our souls, the women we are in God. For twenty-five years we have polished each other like silver, with soft cloths, with loving attention. Birthday gifts fly between us in November and December. We celebrate on the 29th of those two months, ten years apart in chronology as we are. Daily phone calls punctuate times of stress or crisis, or to reassure and comfort. Letters, photographs, poems, flow through the mails. (I'm now trying to convince Madeleine about the speed and convenience of electronic mail!)

Vacations together open up new horizons for both of us. We've driven the Canadian Rockies and, together with our close friend Barbara, been pilgrims to Ireland and Iona and Lindisfarne. We've shopped Fortnum and Mason's in London, and boated across silver Lake Windermere between the green velvet hills of England's Lake District. These tales of travel all end up somewhere in a journal, or a book, or a poem, or serve as grist for reminiscence together.

And so the conversation continues—at the dining room table, the editorial desk, the Table of Communion, and, when we're in the mood for play, even the ping-pong table!

Madeleine's Candlesticks

Zabar's, a New York Saturday morning, I bought
a box of rosy pillar candles, stacked
like quadruplets in the womb, for her four

silver candlesticks which stand, flanking
the orange tulips at table center, tall
and elegant as Madeleine herself. Flames

have danced their highlights on the
visiting faces around the oval table ever since
the sterling quartet was willed to her.

Every visit I search the kitchen for
the soft cotton rags and the clay-colored polish
(a favor; her maid "doesn't do silver").

One afternoon, buffing away, I noticed her name,
misspelled "Madeline," etched dark and faint
along one elliptical base. I knew then I was polishing

not just her treasures but my friend, burnishing
with the well-worn cloth of friendship her silver
self, lifting the light tarnish of time and wear.

Like my shining her words into their
places in her books; like her lighting
blooms of fire in a thousand shadowed minds.

Luci

Dear Madeleine,

It was wonderful to be with you again, even for five days. This is my thank-you note for the warmth of your welcome. It was a good time for both of us, I think. We got a lot of solid work done, because it was quiet and we didn't have a million other commitments and distractions.

Maybe you and I hunger with even more intensity for such quiet times and the private and honest friendship they nurture because so much of our work includes lecturing, teaching, and somehow being "public" persons. The risk is that often we are put on a pedestal, and people who see us thus want to "know" us in a way that they just can't. That pedestal looks mighty attractive to those who aren't on it, and are unaware of the perils of pride and the temptations to arrogance and superiority!

Those who look up to you in adoration want you to be God-like—all-wise, all-knowing, all-loving. And no human being has that capacity; the expectations are unreal, and a kind of idolatry results. Which is why, though I love you, I don't adore you. I know you too well!

And you know me well enough (and still love me) that I can voice my most disturbing doubts and questions about God, and life, and you won't be shocked or put out. I know I won't be dropped from your life like a hot potato. And you, on your part, can make radical theological statements with which I may disagree, but again, because of our bond of love we accept each other for who we are, flawed and failing, but always truth-seeking. I've seen you angry and frustrated, even quixotic. You've seen me depressed and badly misguided or mistaken. But we can talk through these personal glitches and forgive, and come out stronger for the struggle. We can move forward together; we learn compassion for our friends' mistakes when we've made a few ourselves.

The most humbling thing of all is to fall into the same mistakes for which we've denounced others. When I'm tempted to be critical of my mother, I am brought up short by the realization that I use many of her expressions, and exhibit some of her attitudes, expressions, and idiosyncrasies. When I feel critical of others, I usually come to the conclusion that it is because I am guilty of the same inadequacies or irritating habits. But that's how we learn true compassion. Thank you for letting me learn this lesson along with you.

God bless you, my dear friend. This note sent with much love, and gratitude.

Luci

Please Listen In...

As we began to work together on this book we decided to spend time whenever we could, often traveling across the country to be together, or, when both of us were participating at a writers' conference, simply talking about friendship. Of course, we began with conversations about our own friendship but from this we widened the circle to include reflection about others who are important in our lives.

We decided the easy way to go was to tape our conversations as "grist for the mill." Our dialogues, rather than making us feel self-conscious about our friendship, helped the friendship by making it even more intentional, a matter of choice and purpose, rather than mere circumstance or coinciding schedules.

We spent many hours this way, happily talking when Madeleine was stuck in bed after knee surgery, or over dinner, or simply at lunch, eating our tuna sandwiches. In reading over the transcriptions of our tapes we decided to share some of them with you, just as they are, as a way of inviting you to our table to share in our conversation. We hope our discussions will invite your own thoughts, and widen the circle of friendship.

LUCI: Madeleine, a really important aspect of our relationship—really where we began to get to know each other—arose out of our work together, with you as author, and me as editor, working on all the books we've done together.

MADELEINE: Nine books over twenty-five years. And we've survived it! We haven't always agreed. I've sometimes had to fight you over theology...

LUCI: ...And I've had to fight you! We've had vigorous discussions, and violent disagreements. Often I've tried to keep you from going too far out on a theological limb. You like to disturb—to jog people out of their conventional thinking, but I didn't want them to be so irritated and angry that they'd stop listening to you. I knew what you had to say was important, even vital.

MADELEINE: I think what made Hugh's work as an editor for me work so well has also worked for you and me. We, too, had our battles when he was editing my books, but what made it okay was that the ground under our feet was the same ground.

LUCI: I really love you, and you know it. And you respond with love. Having the same ground under our feet — our love for God, God's love for us — is a wonderful basis for both our professional and our personal relationship.

MADELEINE: There's mutuality and meaning in both.

LUCI: I love the way you probe and explore, both in our conversations and in your writing. As your friend and editor I want your writing to come out in the best possible way, so there's nothing of malice or jealousy in my battles with you. Any disagreement is because of the desire on both our parts to make each book the best and truest it can be, and sometimes we see this in different ways. But in the process of the fights and the argumentative discussions, I think we've both learned a lot, about each other, about our convictions, and about how to work together.

MADELEINE: Oh, I agree. We each, in the thick of the moment, are convinced that we're right and the other is wrong. But as we calm down, our minds expand and we each begin to glimpse reality from the other's point of view.

LUCI: That kind of discussion is productive because we learn from ourselves, too. We hear ourselves thinking, wrestling through to reality. And often, after a time of thoughtful conflict, we end up meeting in the middle.

MADELEINE: Or, I give in completely. Or you do. Sometimes I'm right and sometimes you're right. But again, what's important is that we stand on the same ground—on the same Rock—*the Rock that is higher than I*—the Rock of Christ. And that makes all the difference. I mean, I couldn't work with an editor whose view of the universe was totally inconsistent with mine.

LUCI: I remember once when we'd worked hard for hours and hours, and right in the middle of a book we looked at each other, grinned, and said, "We need a break. Let's go to the movies."

And do you remember the day of our spontaneous thanksgiving? We were going through page proofs and after finishing three days of solid textual work together we both stood up and sang the Doxology? It wasn't planned. We hadn't said, "Let's sing the Doxology." We just stood up and sang it. And it really was a song of praise to God that together we had done a good job, and in that cooperative, creative work God was being glorified.

MADELEINE: Luci, what do you say we go take a walk and come back and have tea.

LUCI: Lovely.

Widening the Circle:

The elements of friendship

We are all persons in the making
and in a real sense we are
making and re-making one another.
But how often personal relationships
are marred by hasty, partial or
over-severe judgments.
We must help one another,
not judge one another, and
we must leave the final judgment
to the Divine Patience.
One of the greatest promises
in the New Testament is that
we are accepted in the Beloved.
Let us try to be the ministers
of acceptance.

—*Eric Symes Abbott*

Some Personal Reflections

Madeleine

I love introducing my friends to each other. As friends meet friends and become friends the circles form a beautifully linked chain. The friendship that Luci and I have has enriched both of us because of our sharing of friends, because of the marvelous principle of the "transfer of affection."

Throughout my life, I have lived in many circles of friends, each enriching me and widening my own vision. These circles of friends are sometimes interlocking, with a few seemingly isolated. But, the story isn't over yet and our understanding of the connections is still growing.

From a rather friendless childhood I moved to wonderful circles of friends in boarding school. I then went on to Smith College and the circle widened. I made friends among the people in my house, in my classes, and with those interested in theater. I started a small writing group.

On my first Sunday at college I went to the Episcopal church. Not one person spoke to me. As church had been mandatory in both my English and American boarding schools, I decided I was through with the church establishment. I don't know whether my friends had similar experiences, but not one of us went to a church, of any denomination, to temple or synagogue. Perhaps we needed time out to do some thinking on our own. Mostly our religion had been taught to us by parents, preachers, authorities. This time of exploration was good for me. I'm not sure how I would have fared had I been sent to a "Christian" college.

The circle of friends I built up was ecumenical, to say the least: Christian, Jew, and one Buddhist. Mostly we talked about the play we were working on. We did a truly excellent production of Chekhov's *Three Sisters*. We discussed the literary magazine and how much should be fiction and how much nonfiction. We were serious. We cared about our education.

I had entered college in the autumn of 1937, still in the Great Depression, and most of us looked down on the rich girls because we felt they were lowering the standard of education. We were aware of what was going on in Europe and frightened by it; I had listened to my father coughing his lungs out from that earlier World War, and I was terrified of war, and yet not quite a pacifist. My more politically oriented friends kept me informed about what was going on in the world, the danger Hitler was to all of us, the horror of his hatred of the Jews. All my little circles during college converged, and each one changed me in some way and helped me to grow.

I learned there were people I couldn't trust, and that some people were inherently gossips in a judgmental and sometimes vindictive way. There were people who lied in order to demean someone else. It was probably late for me to learn this, but learn it I did, and was staggered by it.

After college when I went home to New York to write, to work in the theater, my circles changed and expanded. I was profoundly innocent in a world that had lost its innocence long ago. One small circle was an unexpected one: young men who had barely spoken to me during school holidays in the south (where I was the Yankee cousin) came through New York on their ways to overseas assignments. They were lonely, filled with bravado and fear, and I was someone they knew, a real New Yorker! They took me to the Rainbow Room, the St. Regis Room; we met under the clock at the Biltmore. They belonged to a circle that was peripheral, if a circle can be peripheral. I enjoyed the elegance, the rather frenzied playing, because nobody knew how long we were going to be able to play. I corresponded with a few of them when they went overseas, deeply with one who was also a cousin.

I shared an apartment in the Village with three other girls, and worked on my first novel, which had been started in college. My circle of friends was artistic, mostly made up of people who worked in the theater. Our love of theater was passionate and idealistic. We wanted to open windows for a spiritually sluggish world. What does it say that I looked for this in the theater rather than the church? Some of my theater friends were quiet churchgoers. I was not yet ready to return to the institution. I read theology. I prayed. I had never felt isolated from God, only from the institution which seemed too often to confuse itself with God. The God of the institution seemed to be more punitive than the nastiest of my nasty headmistresses. The God I prayed to was God who gave life and love in a world full of death and hostility.

I had my first novel published, a novel largely about vocation, a young pianist moving into her life's work. In a play in which I was the understudy, I met my husband, the young leading man. My husband had had a strict Baptist upbringing, where the arts were considered irrelevant if not outright sinful. In spite of Hugh's degree in theater from Northwestern, his parents gulped and took it bravely when he moved to New York and the theater. They then graciously accepted the blow of his choosing an Episcopalian for a wife, for I was still an

Episcopalian, even if a non-churchgoing one. A marriage which did not include the magnificent language of the Book of Common Prayer hardly seemed valid to me.

We married and had children and our friends were largely theater people, musicians, painters, and writers. Then came a totally different circle. We left the theater and the city and moved to a small dairy farm village in order to bring up our children in a healthy atmosphere. Through friends who had already made this major move, we started going to the Congregational church in the village, and for the nine years we lived there this was our circle, the center of our lives. I loved the circle of friends we made, all of whom were deeply involved in the Congregational church. Both Hugh and I had grown enough not to expect the impossible of our institutions. We believed that our love of God had to be expressed in a public commitment. Our children grew up in a Christian community in a village where most people were either Yankee Congre-gationalists or Polish Catholics. There wasn't much chance for anti-Semitism or racism in this republican little village. I learned a lot in this circle. I still have friends among the people who taught me the intricacies of freezing and canning, and of keeping house—I had never lived in a real house before, only apartments or dormitories.

After nine years, during which we built up a dead general store into a reasonable business, we moved back to New York and the theater. By now church was part of our lives. Our chil-dren were given excellent scholarships in a small Episcopal school, so we thought it was consistent to find and go to the local Episcopal church. But the local Episcopal church did not welcome my husband at the altar; he had made the move from the Baptist to the Congregational Church, and in 1960 many

Episcopal churches practiced "closed communion." This struck me as outrageous! The institution was making God's choices again.

We discovered the Cathedral, less than a mile away from us, where all seekers were welcome at Communion. Our children's school's Christmas pageant had outgrown the school's facilities and was going to be held at the Cathedral, and my husband and I were asked to be the directors.

Our circles were many: the theater, the school, the Cathedral; our friends were drawn from each. The school and the Cathedral were already integrated, before we had begun to look at the ugly face of racism. Our diversity enriched us: walk down any street and you could hear a dozen languages and see people who had come from all over the world.

By now I had half a dozen or more books published and I began to be asked to speak at librarians' conventions, at schools and colleges. One day the phone rang and I was asked by a pleasant-sounding professor if I would speak at a conference on the arts at Wheaton College. The only Wheaton College I had ever heard of was in New England. When the letter came confirming my acceptance it turned out that this Wheaton was in Illinois and was one of the best known of the "Christian" colleges. Someone explained to me that Wheaton was Evangelical. "What's that?" I asked.

Hard to believe, isn't it, that I was in my mid-forties and had never heard of the Evangelical world, knew nothing of its specialized language or the exuberance of its faith. When I was young the Episcopal church was quietly devout; the Congregational church was firm and practical. However, in a way our village church had helped prepare me for Wheaton. The church had no Book of Common Prayer to provide structure;

it was centered on the word, on the Bible, on preaching. I grew up in a biblically literate circle, so there was continuity for me, but at Wheaton the public speaking about faith, which for me had been intensely private, was new and startling. My first visits to Wheaton and other Evangelical colleges were revelations to me.

Perhaps the most important widening of my circle came from the immediacy of prayer, of laying on hands and praying for whomever had need. Not long ago at a conference, a couple about to move to South America with their two young children asked if I would pray with them. Then and there. And I was able to do so, with joy, realizing that this ability to touch and pray was not always mine. Before my circles included the Evangelical world I would have frozen up with shyness, incapable of such an intimate act of spontaneous prayer. There are things about the Evangelical world I find questionable, but even when I most passionately disagree with a theology that includes a punitive and angry God, I am forced into thinking, examining. In an argument, both sides can find scriptural proof for conflicting opinions, but that is a challenge. I know that God loves me, and that he loves whoever is disagreeing with me, too.

Within these wider circles the smaller ones continue. My father died when I was seventeen; my mother lived to be ninety. I loved introducing her to my friends at college, several of whom called her "Aunt Madeleine." Later she became friends with many of my friends, and this sharing delighted me. When she was older, sometimes difficult and crotchety, and would insist on a tray in her room rather than joining the dinner guests, I would say, "Mother, I really need your help. I've got things I have to do in the kitchen, and I can't just leave the guests alone in the living room. Can't you please go in and hold the fort for just a few minutes?" She would oblige, and become the belle of the evening.

In New York I have the double circle of the great Cathedral of St. John the Divine and the smaller circle of my parish church, where I go on Sunday. I am at the Cathedral all week, where I am volunteer librarian. I usually go to the noon Eucharist, where there is a circle within a circle, a group of people who meet together daily to share bread and wine. On Sunday I go to a small parish church, All Angels, which is totally different from the high grandeur of the Cathedral. We don't even meet in a church building (the great old church had to be sold) but upstairs in a room in what was once the parish house. It is a congregation small enough so that we can know each other by name. Probably three-quarters of the worshipers have come from Evangelical backgrounds and have fallen in love with the liturgy. There are a few of us "cradle Episcopalians" and there is a wonderful sense of family. We do a lot of singing. Some of us are "charismatic" and some not and it doesn't matter; we are still one. Most of the congregation is young; we are a wonderfully mixed bag. We are "low church" as it is called, and I love "high church," but this church is alive, questioning, enthusiastic. It is a circle in which I am happy and that first visit to Wheaton was part of what prepared me for this. One circle formed another.

On Sunday mornings I sometimes fix a pot of some kind of stew, not knowing how many people will be coming home for lunch. It is a delight to introduce friends visiting New York to friends from the parish. It is another way of forging that beautifully linked chain: circle to circle to circle. We are linked together and strengthen one another through the friendships we make, and share.

Luci

My circle of friends was carefully restricted by my parents until my growth beyond adolescence allowed me to grow gradually into the new identity and the separation from birth family necessary for maturity. My early years nevertheless included some memorable individuals whose influence in my life lasts to this day. One of these was Cathy Nicoll—"Nicky," to thousands of campers in Canada. She was more than a dynamic camp director to me. She had striking white hair, even in early middle age, a strong, merry face, bright blue eyes, and a resilient spirit. Music and humor burst from her continuously. She taught leadership skills by example as much as by precept, and many of Nicky's girls are leaders today in their own churches and communities across the continent.

She was the one who painted my name in Gothic script on the blade of my first canoe paddle. She shielded me from parental wrath after I'd cut my bangs *really* short during my first two weeks at camp. She encouraged my diving and swimming skills (I won first prize for my back dive one year) and with her help I gained my Red Cross lifesaving medals. She nourished in me an enthusiasm for loving God, the Bible, music, the out-of-doors. My abiding love for nature, tenting, canoeing, adventure, were fostered at Pioneer Camp, under her direction.

Nicky is alive today, still silver-haired and smiling, still resilient in spirit well into her 90s. I visited her in Edmonton last winter, while I was leading a journal retreat at a nearby campground, and she affirmed and astounded me by her spoken wish that were she fit to travel she could "sit under my ministry" and learn from me, when I still feel that I have so much to learn from her. Never married, she recently received the Order of

Canada for her lifetime of work with young people.

The circle widened. A young man with whom I went to Bible College in Toronto introduced me to the symphony and the glory of orchestral music. Though I'd taken piano lessons for years at home, I'd never been to a concert. With him I experienced great orchestras performing Brahms, Saint-Saens, Rimsky-Korsakov. I can't hear some of their symphonies today without fond memories of David.

Going away to Wheaton College in the U.S. further widened my circle. I met young people from other Christian backgrounds, and realized how atypical my church and family life had been. For the first time I developed a wonderful circle of friends, both men and women, of my own choosing. And teachers. My greatest encourager was Dr. Clyde Kilby, a teacher whose name is still invoked by hundreds of his former students, for opening up the windows of their imaginations. After trying out five different majors (to prepare for service as a missionary, the role my parents had picked out for me as the pinnacle of achievement) I took a required English Lit. course with Dr. Kilby, and I knew I was home at last. I declared an English major.

When my father heard of my decision to study English rather than anthropology or Christian Education, he flew to Wheaton and told Dr. Kilby in no uncertain terms, "I don't want you to disturb my daughter's missionary vision!" Quietly Dr. Kilby replied, "Dr. Deck, I have a feeling it's *your* vision, not Luci's!" Of course he was right.

With fellow students I'd meet for honors seminars in the Kilbys' home, and be fed Mrs. Kilby's famous apple turnovers. I got involved as art editor of the literary magazine, as reporter for the school paper and yearbook, and after three years graduated with high honors in Literature, with a minor in New Testament Greek. I'm a writer today largely because of Dr. Kilby's influence; though not himself a poet, for years his valuable critiques influenced my poetry. Later, after my father's death, Clyde relished being known as the honorary grandfather of our five children. We named our youngest daughter Kristin Kilby after him.

Like the waves created when pebbles are thrown into a pond, the circles move out from their center. In the late 1960s, Harold left Moody Bible Institute, where he had been director of the correspondence school, and later, manager of publications, including Moody Press, and we began our own publishing firm which plunged me deeper into the worlds of writing and publishing. We started small, in our own home, with Harold handling finances, sales promotion, and publicity. I not only edited the manuscripts, but got bids for typesetting and printing, and supervised book production, working with gifted book designers. The first year we released three books. I edited manuscripts during the day, and typed up invoices in the evenings, while Harold and the children packed books in our basement warehouse, then filled mail sacks with cartons of books which I took to the post office next morning in our station wagon.

It was satisfying work. Many of our authors became our dear friends. The growth of a book is almost like that of a baby. A gestation period of nine months to a year, then publication, and introduction of this new work to a waiting world! Every year, we attended the Christian Booksellers Association convention, an incongruous mix of commercialism and integrity, like any business enterprise. Harold and I decided early on that the almighty dollar would not be our god, that we would publish books to strengthen faith and open minds and challenge readers whether or not we achieved huge commercial success. We never wanted to build an empire. We liked our independence from denominational or organizational ties. No one was looking over our shoulder, telling us what, or what not, to publish. I started the Wheaton Literary Series—books of quality poetry, fiction, and biography by gifted writers whose worldview was God-centered—though the risk of failure for such books was high in a subculture that had devalued poetry and literary fiction by ignoring it or considering it peripheral. Shaw Publishers continues to be respected in the industry today. I'm still as involved as I want to be, and thankful to Steve Board, the new president, for his leadership of the small enterprise Harold and I started nearly thirty years ago. Seeing Shaw Publishers succeed on its own is like sending your adolescent out into the world, confident of its ability and potential.

During Harold's illness from lung cancer, we grew a new circle—prayer friends who came regularly, week by week, to ask for God's healing help. Some of them had themselves been healed from cancer through prayer. The McDermotts, the Boschs, the Mains, the Lobs, the Kuehns—all of them became friends of the heart as we dug down together into the realities of life and death, learning from each other as we prayed, feeling the blessing of their sacrificial giving of time and energy in prayer. Harold was not healed physically; he died in January of 1986. But his spirit was healed of all bitterness or regret, and he was strengthened emotionally and spiritually through prayer so that we both felt that he was not dying into death, but dying into life.

After Harold's death I was invited to become Regent College's writer in residence. Regent is a graduate school of biblical studies in Vancouver, Canada. There I was welcomed and valued, a healing experience in a time of emotional limbo for me, when I was unsure of my future direction. There I met scores of highly motivated men and women, teachers and staff and students, whose vision of strengthening the laity of the church by theological training of professionals in other fields included an emphasis on the humanities. Regent still gives me this sense of a healing, motivating community where I feel at home.

After I met and married John Hoyte and moved to California, a move which I could never have anticipated in my wildest dreams, I left many long-standing friendships behind in the Midwest. But, thanks be to God, over the past five years I have found many new ones: in my church, Holy Trinity, Menlo Park, with the women in my prayer group; with the friend in Vancouver, a writer and teaching companion, in whose faxes to me in Menlo Park and mine to her, essays and poems are critiqued and sharpened; in the journal classes I teach around the Bay area (my students teach me much as they share their lives and writings); in the members of the monthly discussion group which John and I host. The circle includes sailing friends, camping friends, writer and artist friends, all of whom have enriched and enlivened my California life. And my circle keeps widening. As I travel to teach, lead retreats and workshops, attend board meetings, read poetry, encourage other artists and writers in their callings, I find new friends, and am enlarged and warmed in the process.

Pure friendship is an image of the original and perfect friendship that belongs to the Trinity, and is the very essence of God.

—Simone Weil
Forms of the Implicit Love of God

Letter From Vancouver

Dear Luci,

Hello from the beautiful Pacific Northwest. I'm sending this to you at home in California where I think maybe you are. We are both much too peripatetic. I have been thinking a lot about *Friends for the Journey*, which is, I guess, our latest title for the book. I'm still having trouble with some of the basic definitions and we need to talk soon.

A story. A few years ago our bishop went on a preaching mission to the part of India the apostle Thomas is said to have Christianized. He was wonderfully well received and at the end of his time there he wanted to thank his enthusiastic audience in their own language. So, he turned to his interpreter and asked him for the words for "thank you." The interpreter was puzzled. He went to another interpreter and they consulted. Then, he turned to the bishop and said: "In our language we don't quite have a word for 'thank you' in this way. 'Thank you' is something you do."

I wonder, in our language do we really have an adequate word for friendship? Perhaps this is one of those things about which you can say: "You'll know it when you see it."

I think maybe it is something that you do. Well, at least it is something that *we* do.

I love and miss you.

Madeleine

> A flower is relatively small. Everyone has many associations with a flower—the idea of flowers. You put out your hand to touch the flower—lean forward to smell it—maybe touch it with your lips almost without thinking—or give it to someone to please them. Still—in a way—nobody sees a flower—really—it is so small—we haven't time. To see takes time, like having a friend takes time.
>
> —Georgia O'Keeffe

Take Time; Make Time

Madeleine

Friends take time in a world of shortcuts, instant coffee, fast foods. Yes, it takes time to make friendship, as it does to cook a special meal for those we love. We're surrounded by substitutes and instant gratification and we're offered chemical white stuff to put into instant coffee, and the store shelves are filled with instant cake mixes and instant mashed potatoes. On television we see instant love. But friendship, like all fine things, needs time for ripening. We need to believe in it, knowing that we are all human creatures who make mistakes, even with (or perhaps *especially* with) those we love most. We need forbearance and patience and love.

One day I took my mother-in-law's infallible recipe for moist chocolate birthday cake and set about making a cake for the birthday of one of my little grandsons. While the cake was baking we hung balloons and brightly wrapped presents in the apple trees. Then it was time to frost the cake and I made the mistake of using my own recipe for frosting, rather than my mother-in-law's. My recipe is wonderful: one stick of butter, one box of dark brown sugar and one full square of Baker's chocolate. Delicious, yes, but too heavy for the delicate cake, which began to break apart like ice floes in the spring. I sent the older children scurrying to gather daisies, lots of daisies, and tucked them here and there around the parts of cake, thus holding it all together. It looked a little unusual with its flower face, a little lopsided, but it was delicious, and it certainly had been a labor of love. Like friendship, it took time and patience. It was worth it—and I am still teased about it.

Elements of Friendship

Luci

There are all kinds of words that describe how people relate today. "Relationship" is a catch-all word, so broad it is almost meaningless. "I'm ready for a new relationship," blurts a lonely young person looking for romance. That says very little about lasting commitment or trust. "Networking" and "peer associations" and "connections" are three words often used in the professional world of business. To me they all seem cold and empty, even calculating—words that tell of advantages I intend to gain from you in order to speed my climb up the corporate ladder, or references that would look good on my resumé. Self-absorbed, myopic words, they seem blind to the idea of the warm bonding of kindred spirits that comes with commitment. Such words reflect the fragmentation of humanity in self-protective singleness that shuns the risk of relationship for fear of betrayal or hurt. The idea of giving yourself to someone else in kindness, for the other's benefit, has almost evaporated in the hot friction of our mobile society.

But God never meant us to be separate islands in a sea of loneliness. I think that's why Adam and Eve were given to each other. The animals, fascinating and diverse as they were, couldn't provide the level of friendship that was needed by human beings. We were all created with the ability, the *need* to reach out, to join ourselves with others, in love, to feel *with* and *for* others. The words *sym-pathy* (with-passion) and *em-pathy* (in-passion) both tell a story. We are to stand alongside our friends, entering into their passionate struggles and trials and triumphs, feeling their pangs of pain and the brimming over of their pleasure. Mirror-ing back to them, sometimes, their better selves, when they need our affirmation and encouragement. Giving them permission to mirror back to us our less attractive attributes, so that we can better "see ourselves as others see us" and work on personal transformation, with God's help.

One of the joys of both my life and Madeleine's is that, during writers' workshops or journal-writing workshops, the members of our groups open up their personal lives to us and to each other, often revealing their most intimate realities both painful and joyful. And when this is true, and we enter into each other's emotions, the door is open for true friendships. Many ongoing writers's groups and journal circles spring from those workshops where strangers become friends who want to meet and share their lives and their writing on a regular basis.

Prayer is an important part of such groups. When we enter the new dimension of prayer together we gain deep insights into each others' needs and strengths. Conversely, when we know each other, and are committed to friendship, our prayers become profound and real. They become a natural and valued part of getting together. And if prayer is natural in the ordinary course of human events, think how vital it becomes in crisis! When we have together built a path of prayer to God in time of tranquillity, it will be immediately available to us in life-and-death situations.

Time together is another significant element. Friendship doesn't develop overnight, although we may immediately feel the attraction and potential of a new acquaintance. But it is only after we've been lovingly together for a span of time, and have lived some history to base our trust upon, that our friendship puts down deep roots and becomes something we depend on and invest in. During his public ministry, Jesus had only three years to fulfill his own human need for companionship and to build the friendships that gave the fledgling church its leadership. But think of the consistency of those friendships— of being together with Jesus, day in, day out, in all kinds of circumstances. A kind of envy possesses me, as I think of the disciples. I know that by faith I have the help of God the Holy Spirit, but to have had Jesus as my friend, with skin on, with his voice tones and personal mannerisms and unique, memorable facial features... and then I remember that I *do* meet Jesus in the flesh, as I hear him speaking from the mouths of my friends, as his love wraps me round in their hugs, their letters, their phone calls, their laughter, their tears.

Such friends are easy to be with. They bring out the best in us, and in our conversations and joint efforts each sparks fresh ideas which contribute to the strong bond, and we come away from our times together refreshed, stimulated, affirmed, and feeling happy about who we are. Other friendships may take persistence to breach the old barriers of silence, shyness, or fear, so that love may flow back and forth with freedom.

In tested friendships the words "faithfulness" and "loyalty" assume their true dimensions, because even fast friends can annoy, or irritate, or misunderstand each other; they can even betray or deny each other, as did Judas, or Peter. But where there's loyalty enough to make the knot in a friendship worth untangling, friends can be lovingly honest with each other to the point of resolution and forgiveness. Judas failed to reach that point, but Peter, his heart breaking, confessing and reaf-firming his love for Jesus, was transformed from his immaturity and cowardice to the boldness and power which was the rock of the early church.

When I moved from Illinois to California to marry John Hoyte and make a new life with him, I knew virtually no one in my new setting. But soon after I'd moved I was invited to join a prayer group of four kindred spirits, women who had public ministries as gifted church leaders or therapists, but who needed peers, friends of the heart at the real and intimate level which allows for deep prayer and total honesty. We have been meet-ing together now for five years, and I pray that our closeness may continue into the unknown future. Without such friends, and the even longer closeness with friends like Madeleine, I might have often fallen prey to depression and despair. Here is where the idea of covenant is fleshed out—in our commitment to be to our friends what they need us to be, regardless of circumstances, and to know that they will return the compliment.

When we go to the Lord's Table with a friend, to partake of the eucharistic feast, the comm-union (*together-one-ness*) which we find with each other and with God makes the friendship a sacred trust which death will not erase or nullify.

True friendship means both giving and receiving—giving without obligation, receiving without guilt. This is a way we can move out of self-absorption, which can become morbidly toxic, into a profound, redemptive awareness of others. How do I know when a friendship is true and deep? If it is close enough that I can confidently call the friend at midnight or 3:00 A.M., knowing I'll be listened to and responded to without a second thought. It's accepting responsibility for the friend's welfare. Which really means that in that friend we are also being responsible toward God, and in the long run, to the universe. I consider it a profound compliment if Madeleine calls me at night, like that. It means that *I'm* considered her special, trustworthy friend. And to be a part of such a friendship is an honor.

Friendship means frequent phone calls, letters, face-to-face visits—staying in touch. Because without that *touch*, that contact, we'd feel isolated, and we'd be neglecting a person who is precious to us. We live in a world that for all its communications systems is woefully out of touch with its component parts. When I preached my son's wedding sermon last year I talked about the power of love to heal this wounded world, to form a web of affection and caring that draws us together rather than rending us apart in suspicion or animosity. (Our word *diabolical* comes from the Greek word which means *to tear apart*.) True friends like each other, but they must also really love each other. "If you love me, show it by doing what I've told you," says Jesus. And "You are my friends, if you do the things I command you." One of the things he commands us is that we "love one another" the way he has loved us.

How did Jesus model true friendship? By loving his friends (and us) for who they were and as they were—flawed, forgetful, naive, and often ungrateful. He loved them in action as well as emotion. Though Jesus' feelings for his friends ran deep and strong (think of his tears for Lazarus), though his humanity allowed for sentiment, his friendship never descended to sentimentality. It was never cheapened by empty platitudes. As he said to them, and to us: "Love one another, as I have loved you."

And we have tried, Lord. And we do try. And we will continue, with your help, in your Spirit.

Facets of Friendship:

A variety of gifts

In *Winnie the Pooh*, Rabbit talks endlessly to Piglet about the multitude of his "friends and relations." One gets the sense of vast mob, of crowd. But true friendships happen one by one. Each relationship has its own particularity. Friendship is a multifaceted concept, and each of the many ways of being friends has its own joys, rewards, and responsibilities. In these next pages we explore some of the facets of friendship.

Friendly Word-Play

MADELEINE: In my etymological dictionary I found that the word for friendship is derived from the Middle English "frend" which in turn is derived from the Old English "freond"—the contraction for "freo-gin," to love.

LUCI: So friendship is a special kind of love.

MADELEINE: But maybe we need a new word—something halfway between "acquaintance" and "friend."

LUCI: With a real friend there's an assumption that the friend has an appreciation of the inner you, not just the outer you, the part that's accessible to just about everyone.

MADELEINE: On the phone the other day my secretary refer-red to somebody as my "close, deep friend," and I said, "No! That's not so!" That's an assumption that people jump to fairly often if they have been acquainted with each other for a while, or see each other fairly often in the line of work. Such contact doesn't automatically mean close, deep friendship.

LUCI: There are so many good people, fine people, with whom one will remain an acquaintance forever without ever achieving the intimacy which signals real friendship, and which makes one vulnerable. Long-term connection doesn't guarantee anything in terms of the heart connection we mean when we refer to someone as *a real friend*.

MADELEINE: That's why we need some new word—something between "acquaintance," which is casual, a mere recognition of the outer person, and "friend," in which we acknowledge and value and understand the inner person. Any suggestions?

Madeleine's Journal Entry

Luci has just left and we had a marvelous few days together, talking, cooking, eating, going to the noon Eucharist at the Cathedral. Are we any further on Friends for the Journey? *We think so, and this afternoon we had an excellent conversation about intergenerational friendships. We talked about the fact that most of my friends in New York are younger than I am. Well, maybe there is something statistical in this. Aren't most people younger than I am?*

Luci has never been to one of my traditional slumber parties in December, and I told her about them in some detail. She thinks the parties are a wonderful example of the joys of intergenerational friendships and I said I would write it out for the book.

The tradition began early one December when Gloria was reluctantly turning seventy. She's a beautiful woman, a Southerner, charming and quirky. She hated the idea of being seventy (though I told her I had done it years before and it seemed safe to me) and she berated herself for letting it slip out. So a group of us, friends who had known each other for a long time, retaliated by giving her a slumber party.

Since it was Gloria's birthday party, she got the guest room. Marilyn, in her sixties, got the sofa bed. Leslie, in her fifties, had the fold-out cot, and Carole, also in her fifties, got the tiny "maid's bedroom" in the back, which hasn't held a maid in our tenure. Sandy, the youngest of us, in her forties, slept on the blow-up mattress. We had an absolutely wonderful time, and the fact that we represented four decades didn't make the slightest difference. In fact, I think it enriched the stew.

When Luci and I talked about this, she said the reason I am able to have young friends is because I don't hold on to the past in a restrictive, dogmatic way, announcing that everything about the present is terrible the way some people do, especially those of my age. I certainly hope I don't. A lot about the present is terrible, but my young friends think so too.

There's been more change in this century than in all the centuries preceding it, and while in some areas we've made a lot of progress, we're also in a mess with racism and sexism, drug abuse and child abuse, and so on and so on—things we ought to have grown up enough to be better about. I suppose terrorism has always existed, pirates on the sea and highwaymen, but the terrorism of blowing up a plane or gassing a subway seems more appalling, maybe because it's more impersonal and affects a larger number of people.

Thank God for younger friends who don't think we are passé or outmoded or can't understand the way people think today. Thank God they let us be who we are.

And, they expect me to be able to do everything they can do—such as walk the fifty blocks from the apartment to Lincoln Center. I guess that means they're not thinking of me as an old dodderer even when my knees give way.

Luci told me that she went for a strenuous hike in Colorado with her friends, the Philip Yanceys, and she wouldn't have attempted it on her own because of her weak ankle. She loved it! Recently she hiked with her prayer group on a steep, rocky path down a thousand feet into the Canyon de Chelly in Arizona and then back up again. They are (somewhat) younger and she said their energy kept her going. Of course, I keep remembering that Luci has gone bungee-jumping in New Zealand, so nothing surprises me!

Though I rejoice in my younger friends, it's also good to have friends my own age. As your body begins to tire a bit, lose its vigor, your joints creak a little and your skin develops age spots and gets less elastic, you know you're not the only one. As someone once said, the greatest aid to celibacy after fifty is nudity!

⁂

Luci's Journal Entry

Waiting at the airport for my plane yesterday I got into conversation with a most interesting woman. She was writing in her journal, which immediately alerted me to her possibilities! Then I noticed on the seat beside her the book I had just finished, and loved, Snow Falling on Cedars. She was younger than I, not conventionally pretty, but with bright brown eyes and an inquiring tilt to her head. We talked for perhaps half an hour, beginning with the book, and going on to discover many things in common, including our love of the Pacific Northwest and camping. She told me she supports herself by photojournalism but she writes poems on the side—says that's the true window of her soul—and she values her husband and children as I do mine. I didn't learn a lot about her spiritual foundations, though she mentioned her involvement in the Methodist church, but just the way she talked, and the way her eyes lit up with warm understanding once we got past the pleasantries, made me think there was real potential for friendship.

Since she was taking a later flight than I, we parted when I had to board my plane. And that was that. There are probably a couple of dozen people I've met and connected with like that over the course of my life. I could call such casual, unplanned touches between two people "fetal friendships"—as full of potential as an unborn baby, but never able to flower into real friendship, miscarrying because of the circumstances of meeting, or lack of time, or other pressures. Two lives glancing off each other, with sparks of warmth and understanding. They're gifts, because they reaffirm our faith in the grace of the unplanned, the unexpected. I think God has these kindred spirits everywhere, hidden, then momentarily revealed, even if in this life they never get the chance to shine brighter than the brief flame of a struck match that goes out when the wood has been consumed.

Who knows? If we're meant to be friends, maybe our paths will cross again!

The Clink of Glasses

MADELEINE: ...and then there's what I call "cocktail party friendships"...

LUCI: ...the endless small talk, in a room shrill with chatter...

MADELEINE: ...that never really connects. If you should ask any of your cocktail party friends for help...

LUCI: Well, that's just not done. You're trying so hard to impress people with your competence and sophistication, you wouldn't ever admit your neediness! What the cocktail party kind of acquaintance means is that you merely clink your bubbles— your plastic shells—as you pass in the crowd. But it's not the accepted thing to address your real feelings. In that kind of situation you can be surrounded by artificially cheerful people, yet feel intensely lonely.

MADELEINE: It's not even acceptable to express real needs and feelings in some churches. Hugh used to say that at the coffee hour the person talking to you was frequently looking over your shoulder to see if there was someone more important he or she would prefer to talk to.

LUCI: What an indictment! Maybe that's why Alcoholics Anonymous is so successful; it fills a vacuum that many churches never acknowledge.

MADELEINE: This is *some* churches mind you, certainly not all. I know of a great many churches where being who you are is actually seen as a gift!

LUCI: We are both fortunate that we are part of church families that are places of warmth and outgoing friendship and help. Our friends in Christ in our churches can address both spiritual and emotional needs. And body too: let us not forget the casserole brigade!

Adventuring Together

Luci

One way Madeleine and I express friendship is by planning and participating in adventures together, be it a trip around the world or a short ride to the recycling center, where one of us just goes along to keep the other company.

I really treasure the dimension of our friendship that has developed in the past few years. When I asked Madeleine what she wanted for her 75th birthday, she immediately said, "Go on a vacation with me!"

So we started to plan for the following spring. We decided not to follow her first impulse—to take a trip on the Orient Express and the Trans-Siberian Railway—not just yet, anyway, until we'd had some practice holidaying with each other. That's when we settled on the trip through the Canadian Rockies, and made some hotel and plane reservations. Madeleine flew out to Seattle, and I picked her up there in a rented car. After spending a few days together with two of my children, Kris and Jeff, at my cabin in Sudden Valley, we drove through the pristine wilderness of northern Washington, and up across the Canadian border, through Kelowna, to Banff.

We had a superb time! Madeleine was still recovering from her surgery for knee replacement, and yet she ventured on a (slow) four-mile hike around Lake Louise, complete with cane. I was impressed by her self-discipline as she regularly did her therapeutic knee exercises while sitting on park benches, or standing by the car door as I loaded or unloaded the trunk—anywhere and everywhere. She was determined to become fully active again, immediately!

Then there was the incident when I accidentally locked us out of the car near Emerald Lake, and we had to hitch a ride with some other tourists so we could make a phone call to AAA to come and unlock our car door. It took hours, but she never complained. She was tired, but a good sport. And we found the greatest little gift shop at Emerald Lake, where she bought me that nifty Aussie hat. And I got her some beads to go with one of her long dresses. But the best gift was the fun of being together, following our noses into new adventures, even misadventures!

One night, during a storm, the power went off all up and down the valley, including the power at our hotel. The maids came to our hotel rooms like vestal virgins, with lighted candles for each of us. But they weren't bright enough to read by, and next morning we both reported to each other that we'd had a hard time settling down to sleep, without our usual routine of reading and relaxing gradually into sleep.

We had mixed weather—snow, sleet, sunshine—but the views were always magnificent, even seen through sheets of precipitation. We also had mixed accommodations. We splurged on a couple of great luxury resorts, and then, to make up for the extravagance, we grunged in some noisy motels without nonsmoking rooms. But it was all fun because of companionship.

The next year we went with our friend Bara to Iona in Scotland, as well as some other holy places in Ireland and England, and then to London to see some plays together with my son, Jeff, who has been living and working in London for several years.

Of course Madeleine had her laptop computer along—as is usual. She's always in the middle of a new novel, or a new book of reflections. And when she goes silent in the middle of a conversation, we know she's suddenly transported by a new plot twist, or an unexpected character, or idea, charging into the action.

We enjoy each other enormously, and respect our mutual need for moments of quiet and privacy, which is why we all have separate rooms in the hotels—we need alone-time as much as together-time. It's all part of the friendship package. Being together, alone. Being alone, together.

The Healing Touch

Luci

My sister-in-law, Geila Bar-David, wrote her doctoral dissertation on the profound and positive changes that occur in one who is the caregiver of a chronically ill or terminally ill friend or member of the family. Geila ought to know; her mother had Alzheimer's, and Geila and her sisters were constantly present—major players in their mother's final days.

Their own qualities of compassion and self-giving were channeled, polished, and strengthened by even the most mundane aspects of health-care and emotional support supplied to their aged parent. They learned, not from how-to books or seminars, but from each other and from their own hearts, how sacrificial caregiving, rather than representing only frustration, fatigue, or personal restriction, became a supreme gift to them.

An important and surprising result from this gift is the sense of meaning and significance gained by the experience of these years; there were few regrets or misgivings and a great sense of gratitude for the new roles that have been played, and the wisdom gained in making such loving caregiving possible.

I experienced much of the same blessing during the sixteen months that I lived with and nursed Harold through lung cancer. Never an easy time; our emotional weather fluctuated wildly with dismal diagnoses or momentary reprieves, but I was enriched with the deepening of my own grasp of life-and-death realities.

During those months I grew in my soul and spirit more than I would have thought possible. In thankfulness: for all the good days of our marriage, for the *now* of each golden moment together. In patience and forbearance: with a much-loved spouse whose malaise after chemotherapy sometimes made him respond with unaccustomed irritation. With appreciation: as he inducted me into the mysteries of our business affairs and investments, and the intricacies of car, or furnace, or machine maintenance, with the goal that when he was no longer with me to help me, I would not feel so helpless. With amazement: as I sensed my newfound decision-making ability burgeoning. With more thankfulness: for the supportive friends and family who tempered my sense of aloneness in the heavy responsibilities of keeping both home and business running smoothly.

When Harold went to heaven, and I was on my own for the first time in many decades, I was well on the way to growing up—at age fifty-nine! The sixteen months of his illness had allowed me—urged me—to make the transition from dependence to independence, from uncertainty to confidence.

My life was also enlarged in caring for others in crisis. When a young married friend asked me to be her coach in the delivery, at home, of her second child (now my goddaughter), I agreed, and began to study the only book I had on hand, about "emergency childbirth." Having been through five births of my own, I felt I knew a good deal about what should happen! A week later she called me to come, on a frigid winter night. Her doctor, a specialist in home births, had not yet arrived, having to travel sixty miles on snow-packed roads to reach his patient. As her labor increased in intensity, and her contractions came closer and closer together, we realized that the doctor might not make it in time. Finally she cried out, "The baby's coming!" The moment of truth was upon us. Quickly the young father and I prayed for God's help in this most wonderful, yet critical, of events. Minutes later, she delivered her baby daughter, squalling lustily, and I had the privilege of guiding this new life into the world, catching the baby, cutting her umbilical cord, and cleaning her up. All the doctor had to do, when he arrived a few minutes later, was weigh her! He told us, "You did it all just right. I couldn't have done it better!"

What a glow of excited joy suffused us all. We'd been part of the miracle. The euphoria was as great as I'd felt at the birth of my own babies. I wouldn't have missed it for anything.

One of the joys of my life has been to take Communion, after church on Sundays, to an elderly woman friend—ninety-six years old—and share with her not only the bread and wine, which has such central meaning to us both, but something of the day's sermon, as well as news of church doings and friends. She has my phone number so she can call me if she needs other kinds of help or information. Recently she slipped into a place of semi-coma and confusion and now needs round-the-clock care. I still take Communion to her, though I doubt if she recognizes me anymore, or understands what is going on. Nevertheless, God is still with us in her room, and his presence and love is the deepest kind of comfort.

The giving and loving that happen when we care for someone close to us transforms us, deepens us, gives us a sense of how God our Father must feel as he cares for us in our need, for which we give him the gratitude of our hearts.

Madeleine

When Hugh's mother was dying, he and his sister, Genevieve, talked on the phone several times daily. I appreciated the fact that Hugh and Genevieve had each other. At that time my own mother was well on in age and her health was fragile. I knew that when my mother was dying I would not have the comfort of a sibling, the opportunity to consult with and make decisions with a brother or sister. I was the daughter, the only child.

Though the decisions were mine, I was not alone. I had the blessing of a husband and grown children to back me up, to help with the caregiving. During my mother's last summer we had a full, four-generation household. It was exhausting, but an inexpressible comfort. I am grateful indeed that it was the very size of the family, packed into our old farmhouse, that enabled me to keep mother at home to die. Also, my own work can be done from home. I have known women who have had to juggle visits to the nursing home with family or jobs.

When my mother was a young woman, there were no nursing homes. Wage earners did not go far from home to do their various jobs. It was natural, then, to grow up in one neighborhood, marry, have children, grow old, and die all in the same town. Caregiving could be, and was, shared by the community.

It's different today. Geographical distances and small living quarters, have changed things, and we're not going back to the old ways. Caregiving, even with those we love most, is becoming more difficult, though no less important. We are not always given the choice of being the caregiver, or of being *able* to be the caregiver. When this responsibility does come, a new expression in an old relationship has to be accepted. At this time we pray for the grace to make the change, and to be aware of the unexpected richness it can bring to our lives.

The Peaceable Kingdom

Madeleine

My dog loves me the way God loves me. Utterly and completely, no matter what I do. If I accidentally trip over the dog, I am immediately forgiven and loved. If I am unhappy, if I cry, my dog is there to comfort, to lick away tears. If I am in any way threatened, my dog is ready to protect.

I have had a number of canine friends, most living to ripe old ages. When the time comes we take the ancient animal to the vet who has known us and our creatures for many years, and we stay with our dog, holding the old body for the few seconds until the shot has had its painless and lethal effect.

A cat's love is different, but we have always had cats and dogs together in a peaceable kingdom. My New York cat, Tatiana, is a beautiful little white princess who came from the Humane Society when she was seven months old but looked no more than seven weeks. It took her quite a while to discover herself and her place. At first she shared the apartment with Kelly and Terrible, who belonged to my granddaughter, and Taty was not at all displeased when those two rambunctious felines moved on to other quarters.

Taty is my first praying cat. I have a small Monday prayer group which usually meets at my apartment. When we gather in a circle to pray, she comes from wherever she is and places herself right in the middle of us. If we do not start to pray as soon as she thinks proper, she comes and sits, looking at us expectantly and sternly.

A larger group of my church friends come once a month with the rector and his wife for dinner, to discuss the problems, joys, and hopes of our church family. We end the meal and the discussion with Eucharist around the table. Taty knows this routine and, as we near the end of the meal, in she comes, ready and, if necessary, urging us to pray.

Animals, too, are part of God's kingdom. My first dog, Touché, crawled with her old and aching bones under the rocking chair where, during the night, I was rocking and nursing my baby boy, not willing to neglect what she felt to be her duty, though she died the next day.

Sarah Crewe, in Frances Hodgson Burnett's *The Little Princess*, is demoted to being a little slave living in a barren attic, and there she makes friends with a rat she calls Melchisedek, who comes to visit her every night.

A little girl, fighting back tears, told me that her pet rabbit had died, and she had been informed that the rabbit could not go to heaven, because rabbits have no souls. I said, "You know what? Only the human creatures were thrown out of the Garden. The animals weren't. I don't think you need worry about your rabbit."

Wasn't the parent or teacher who told the little girl her rabbit could not go to heaven playing God? God made it all, sky and sea, water and land, green growing things and all birds and animals, and called it good, very good.

Who are we more likely to meet in heaven: the person who makes god-like decisions about who is or is not saved, or the loving dog who rescues the baby from the burning house?

Winter nap

Winter afternoon.
A thick quilt.
A meditating cat
sealing the crack of air
between bed and
body. Under
the massage of paws
even the cold, cramped heart
relents, blessed by the prayer of purr.

Luci

God's Beast

Least important of all animals, I am a beast
of burden. I can carry heavy loads,
and I am more patient than a camel,
gentler of nature, though occasionally stubborn.
I am not counted intelligent,
and my name is used as an insult.

But when I see an angel in my path
I recognize a messenger of God.
"Stop!" the angel said to me, and I stopped,
obeying God rather than my master, Baalam,
who hit me and cursed me and did not see
the angel's brilliance barring our way.

Later, I took the path to Bethlehem,
bearing God's bearer on my weary back,
and stood beside her in the stable, trying to share
her pain and loneliness, and then the joy.

I carried on my back the Lord himself,
riding, triumphant, through Jerusalem,
But the blessings turned to curses,
Hosanna into Crucify him! Crucify him!

Least important of all animals, beast of burden,
my heaviest burden is to turn the curse into a blessing,
to see the angel in my path,
to bear forever the blessing of my Lord.

Madeleine

Vive la Différence

Luci

I love my woman friends. Because of our common gender, even our female physiology and psychology, we have a basis for knowing and understanding each other with compassion. We know what it's like to have monthly ups and downs; we may have experienced childbirth, nursed our babies, and gone through menopause with other women, and those experiences all become shared bonds.

But I value my men friends equally, and for different reasons. I really like men, and not only for the humanity we have in common; I find in them a complementarity which, as its name implies, supplies me with an agreeable, surprising sense of completeness. And this applies not only to husbands (and I've had two excellent husbands, Harold, whose death left me alone in 1986, and John, whom I married in 1991). The men I've worked with professionally, as well as my male kindred spirits, remind me of what Jesus, the God-man at the heart of my life, might have been like. In fact, I like to think of the way several women in the Bible were close friends with Jesus—Mary and her sister Martha were as dear to Jesus as their brother Lazarus, perhaps more so. He was thoroughly at home in their home. I think it was ordained by God that Mary Magdalene—a woman—was the first of his friends to see Jesus after his resurrection. Martha, and the unnamed woman at the well in Samaria were, besides Peter, the only recorded individuals who recognized and acknowledged Jesus' messiahship. Clearly Jesus, a man, brought a vital dimension into their lives.

And I see Christ in many of my male friends.

Dorothy Sayers, in her wonderful little book *Are Women Human?* discusses the radical way—for his time—that Jesus related to women. He neither patronized them, despised them, nor ignored them, but he entered fully into their joys and sorrows as one human being with others. And in return they gave him the gift of their loyalty. They weren't "camp followers," in the usual negative sense, but there's evidence that they cared for Jesus' welfare during the days of his public ministry.

I loved reading a biography of Dorothy Sayers, which told of her friendship with Charles Williams. A deep kinship grew between them because he opened up to her a world of the spiritual imagination, which went beyond scholarship and resulted in a flow of invigorating correspondence between them.

Men friends stir me, not sexually, though there's always a gentle undertone of eroticism in any friendship between the sexes. Somehow, with a man, I'm challenged to excel myself, to be the best woman I can be—feminine but not weak or helpless, attractive without being vain or empty-headed, capable of leaps of intuition, but also capable of logical thought. I'm on a number of boards, some of them with a preponderance of business executives, corporate-type men of action. Perhaps I was initially invited onto those boards to supply "the woman's touch," or even to be a "token woman." But I believe I've proved myself of value, contributing as much of the "wealth, work, and wisdom" needed from board members, as my CEO friends. I've certainly learned, in board sessions, to listen carefully, but also to be assertive, even confrontive, when necessary. So I'm grateful for those professional associations, and the men I work with, who have become my friends.

I am refreshed, these days, by the freedom I now have which

was denied me in the church in which I grew up, and in which many years of my married life were spent. Women were to be silent, wearing head coverings as signs of their submission. Though I was traveling and speaking around the continent to other groups of Christian men and women, in my own place of worship my voice was silenced, not allowed to be heard. If I wanted to contribute an idea, I had to whisper it to my husband, who then had to express it on my behalf. One of Harold's greatest gifts to me was his decision to move to the Episcopal church, where we could both be used in public ministry, and where *giftedness* was considered rather than *gender.*

Some of my closest men friends I have come to know in the Chrysostom Society—a group of writers who get together regularly for mutual encouragement and stimulation related to our work. Roughly divided between men and women, we are all there as individuals, not as couples, none of us gaining an identity as the spouse of someone else.

I have grown into a deep spiritual friendship with my rector, with whom I meet for prayer for ourselves and our parish on a regular basis. Another friend of the heart is the writer Harold Fickett. When I was asked by Richard Foster to come as a visiting scholar to Friends University in 1987, to write my book *God in the Dark*, I arrived in Wichita, Kansas in that bleak time when I was still grieving for my husband. Harold Fickett was himself going through a bleak time. We were both vulnerable and lonely. He is twenty-five years younger than I. We never had a romantic relationship. But we did spend much time together.

When I first arrived he gave me the keys to his house and suggested that on free evenings, rather than endure mournful solitude in the little apartment that was mine for those months, I might come over and do my studying or reading while he corrected papers or prepared for the classes he was teaching. It was a salvific decision. We contributed to each other more than our physical presence. We saved each other from despair. There was a good deal of prayer together, of sharing wounds and losses, and celebrating gains. We saw many movies together, listened to music, cooked gourmet meals for each other. There was a lot of book talk and God talk. That was ten years ago, and though circumstances have changed for both of us, he remains one of my closest friends and has grown close to my husband, John, as well.

Of course, spiritual friendships between men and women can be invaded by wrong motivations and become opportunities for the relationship to become compromised. There are sexual boundaries that should not be transcended, and we need to safeguard our moral territory, with God's help.

Men and women? *Vive la différence.* But celebrate our common ground, our humanity.

The Family Tree:

The friends you didn't choose

Roots and Branches

Madeleine

Is there any such thing as a happy family? Tolstoy says not. I've met a few people who've pronounced their dislike of any kind of family at all, particularly of blood relatives. My years have taught me that every family is a mixed bag and a completely happy family would be totally abnormal. I have been greatly blessed in that I loved and respected my parents, and I like my family, most of them, most of the time. I *wanted* children, and grandchildren, as did my husband, and we both rejoiced in them. Blessings all, not to be taken for granted.

My birth family was small, but even with three people the dynamics were never dull. Artistic parents. An only child arriving late in the marriage. New York between two wars, the century already split in two.

My mother was a Southerner, gentle as a steel spring. My father was a "damnyankee," volatile, charming, and slowly dying from mustard-gassed lungs, the result of his service in the First World War. For most of my growing-up life, his health was the focus of much of the family's attention.

My father's work as a newspaper correspondent took him back and forth between the States and Europe, where we sought out climates suitable for his health. When I was twelve, we moved across the Atlantic. He died, finally succumbing to his dreadful illness, when I was seventeen.

By this time, we had returned to the United States and lived with my mother's mother in the town in North Florida where my mother was born and grew up. This meant for me moving from the relative isolation (pun completely unintended) of my childhood into a very large family of colorful people, storytellers all. Almost everybody was a cousin and I never even tried to count them.

My father too had come from a large family. He was the one boy at the bottom of a long line of sisters. Most of my cousins on his side of the family were female, and old enough to be my mother. There were, among them, three sisters, and if I could have hand-picked special cousins I'd have picked them. I didn't get to know them until after college when I was living in New York, working on my first novel and living in the world of the theater. When things got too much for me I'd call them and say—not ask, really—"May I come down for a few days?" They lived in a big old Victorian house outside Philadelphia, and I wrote much of my first novel sitting on their window seat with an old college notebook and a fountain pen.

Inasmuch as it is possible, I "chose" my children. That is, Hugh and I wanted children. When I didn't conceive in three months, I thought I was going to be sterile for life. Wrong. I know that many "surprise" children have been great delights to their parents, but Josephine and Bion were lovingly planned, lovingly conceived, and lovingly birthed.

Then, there was indeed a surprise. Bion's birth nearly killed me, and I had to face the fact that I was not going to give birth to any more babies. But God is full of surprises, terrible and wonderful. Through the unexpected and tragic deaths of two of our close friends, their daughter Maria came into our family as our second daughter. I would have liked half a dozen or so more, but three was probably the right number. Not 2.5, or whatever the correct statistic is, but three, all different, all miracles.

And now there is the miracle of grandchildren, five (I'd like half a dozen or so more of them, too), and nineteen legal godchildren, and quite a few more informal ones. I am like most grandmothers, absurdly and totally in love with my grandchildren, all of whom are unusually beautiful, intellectual, brilliant, et cetera, and of course this is true.

They light my life, these great gifts of love, ranging in age from nine years to the late twenties. The two eldest, girls fourteen months apart, lived with me during their college years; Charlotte was with me for seven years and she and Lena taught me more than any number of advanced degrees. They kept me from falling into any kind of rigid pattern; in many ways they helped give birth to the new me who had to be born when my marriage ended with my husband's death. Nothing can take away the forty years of our love, but life changes radically after the death of a spouse.

My language is probably a little more colorful than it might have been without these two young women. Our discussions about politics, the Trinity, recipes for cooking Afghanistanian food, are delights. There are times when we do not agree, and some of it is (I believe) wisdom learned by living through a great many more years than they have, but the arguments are never bitter; we never try to wipe each other out.

When we all get together, my children and their children,

and I look at this family I didn't choose, the dear ones God gave me, I think that if I could choose my family out of the entire population of the universe, I couldn't choose better.

Luci

As we work together on this book about friendship I am realizing how much Madeleine and I have learned about the positives from what might be considered the negatives. From our lonely (or at least rather solitary) childhoods—she was an only child, I was one of two overprotected siblings—we learned the possibilities of family life well enough to enlarge our spheres when it came time to bear our own children. From the experience of feeling shut off from social popularity, we both probably learned how to be more attuned to the needs of lonely or secluded people. And we have come to appreciate the soul friends whose criteria for friendship are not social graces, money, influence, or power, but loving honesty and integrity.

My mother was forty-six when I, her first child, was born, and my father was sixty. My brother came along nearly three years later. They were older parents even by our current standard. They were still in the Victorian age, class-conscious, and very British. Their values meant private schools for us—schools which certainly provided us with superb educational opportunities.

Their elitism went further than the social and educational. Former missionaries, our parents forbade us, because of their ultraconservative convictions about Christianity, to participate in dances or parties. Cardplaying was, of course, frowned upon. Sunday was more than a day of rest; it was a day so severely restricted that even going for a drive in the country, playing anything but hymn tunes on the piano, reading anything but the Bible, even taking photographs, or knitting, were not allowed. It seemed as if my parents wanted to emphasize our differences from others, and to separate us in order to protect us from any influences that might adulterate our Britishness, our gentility, our legalistic religion, anything that appeared to them "common or unclean." My brother and I tried to question these standards as, perhaps, inconsistent with loving Christian values, but there was always a dogmatic refusal to even discuss the issues.

Though we faithfully attended a small, local church, my brother and I didn't go to Sunday School there, with the children of "working class families." My parents established in our home a Sunday School suited to their own ideals, and invited parents with similar rarefied standards to be the teachers, and bring their children as students. Once again, these were friends I didn't choose.

I was sent to a wonderful Christian camp in the summers, but because my mother considered shorts immodest and pants only for boys, I wore only skirts for canoeing, hiking, and other sports. Once again, even among other Christians, I was made to feel different. As a teenager I could wear no makeup. (I felt daring and guilty when I secretly bought a jar of Noxzema!) I wasn't permitted to date until I went away to college. Though I achieved academic honors in high school, and with them some grudging respect from teachers and peers, I always felt an alien, and often a moody or sullen one at that. I was not a cheerful child. My best friends, the ones I felt akin to, even if they didn't come from pedigreed families, got the freeze treatment at home. Like Madeleine, I found my happiest world in books and music, which opened my imagination to new horizons.

Does this all sound very negative? I know now that my parents' convictions, conservative though they were, were a passionately held reflection of their own upbringing. Overprotectiveness was their way of expressing their devotion to us, the precious children of their old age.

Restrictive though my own upbringing was, there were rewards. We traveled widely—from England, my birthplace, to wild and wonderful places like Australia, and then back and forth between Sydney, and Toronto, Canada. It was in Australia that I was happiest. I had over seventy first cousins there (my Dad was one of twelve vigorously procreative siblings) with whom we went on picnics, spent days swimming at the glorious beaches, and took holidays in the Blue Mountains. These gorgeous landscapes are still imprinted on my imagination. There my love of the wildness of nature increased; there I felt true freedom and the joy of being accepted in a larger group.

But even in our travels we would be plucked out of school in the middle of a term in one country, and dropped into a different educational system in another—wherever our father felt there might be more scope for his conference speaking. He was a restless man as well as a dynamic preacher, and his work kept him away from home for weeks at a time. Dad's blithe assumption was always: "You youngsters are bright; you'll catch up." And we did. But the anxiety level, the stress of leaving familiar settings behind and starting over, and over again, of having an absentee father, was greater than Mother and Dad realized.

I always knew that Dad was immensely proud of us, and of our small achievements. He loved my early poems, and carried them with him to read to friends. An enthusiastic, warm, and demonstrative man, his children were the apples of his eye. We wanted to please him, and doing well in school and living out their patterns of life and faith were what pleased him and Mother most. Pleasing others, to gain approval and security, became a pattern of life for me, a pattern which I am struggling even now to reverse, as I still find myself attempting, from time to time, to please Mother, eight years after her death at ninety-nine.

When I left Canada to attend Wheaton College in the U.S. and met young people from other Christian circles, I was finally able to realize that the life I'd been living wasn't exactly normal. For the first time, I was free to make new friends of my own choosing, some of whom are still close to me today. A wider world was opening.

Five days after college graduation, rather than becoming an overseas missionary as my parents had planned, I married Harold Shaw. In the next six years we had four children. My kids ask me today how I managed—living on the meager income Harold earned at Moody Bible Institute, with me doing freelance editing, tutoring private pupils in New Testament Greek, and correcting exams for Moody Correspondence School, while caring for my small babies and toddlers. My answer: I managed, but raggedly, juggling priorities, with only minor cracks of time in which to write poems. That was when Dr. Kilby, my college mentor, gave me, for my 29th birthday, twenty-nine stamped, self-addressed envelopes—his broad hint that he wanted me to take my poetry seriously enough to circulate it more widely.

As years widened the distance between me and my childhood, I discovered, too, the freedoms of being Spirit-directed rather than being ruled by human legalisms. I saw God through new eyes, not as a restrictive law-giver but the kind of parent, tough but tender, that a child needs and wants, deep down.

We parents do give our genes to our children, but we have little control over their makeup, their personalities, and gifts. We may choose to have children, but even if we are biologically capable of bearing them we have no way of knowing, or choosing, how they'll turn out! There's a lot of trial and error involved, certainly with the first couple of offspring, on whose backs we learn parenting skills by necessity and experimentation.

My children all were, and are, very distinct from each other—Robin, Marian, John, Jeff, Kristin. They are now, as adults in their own right, my best friends, but they certainly put Harold and me to the test as they wrestled their way through childhood and adolescence, to independence! We are bound together by blood, by responsibility, by parental and filial love, by those strong cords inbuilt to preserve the integrity of families. We have little choice about it; it's not *if* we bring up our children, but *how*—how we live out our roles.

And now they are themselves the parents of a new generation—Lauren, Lindsay, Katherine, Michelle, Jack. How quickly the roles reverse! We who were dependent children become the ones depended on. And I know—from the experience of watching my father succumb to leukemia at eighty-three, and my mother grow old and blind, to die opinionated as ever, and always dogmatically certain that she was right, and that if we disagreed with her, we were wrong— that dependence on others lies ahead of us. It may not be what we choose. But we can at least try to learn from past failures, and maintain our grace and dignity as we grow toward heaven in company with friends we choose, and the family we were given.

Eating the Whole Egg
for my great-great-grandfather

Oral history tells us you went through
three wives. One story is that
every day you breakfasted with
your current spouse on toast
and a three-minute egg,
chipping off its white cap in the precise
British way, and in a grand gesture,
spooning to your wife that minor albumen,
watery, pale as her self. That was her meal;
you feasted on yolk, rich and yellow
as a gold sovereign, and crushed the shells,
feeding them by gritty doses to
your offspring lined up along the table—
a supplement to stave off rickets and
accustom the family to patriarchy.
Nourished thus on remnants and rigor,
your tribe multiplied to twenty-two.
The legend astonishes me still. And I
still bear, along with those woman
genes, a vestigial guilt
whenever I cook myself a breakfast egg
and then devour it, white, yolk,
protein, cholesterol, and all. Like
seeing the sun after generations of moons.
Like being the golden egg, and eating it too.

Luci

Thoughts of Home

Madeleine

"Home is the place where, when you have to go there, they have to take you in.... I should have called it something you somehow haven't to deserve." So wrote Robert Frost. Lovely. But is it always true? I hope that whenever anyone in my family turns up, no matter how unexpectedly, or for whatever reason, the welcome mat will always be out.

That was certainly true for the prodigal son, although his elder brother did not share in his heart the loving welcome of the father. What about people who talk about "heaven home"? Is everybody who comes knocking at the door welcome? We've all heard stories of the living room full of family photos, but one is turned to the wall. Whoever was in that picture has been thrown out. Negated. Unwelcome.

I know a woman who is a strict Baptist. (She is a "fundalit," which is a word I created to describe fundamentalists who are biblical literalists—fundamentalist/literalist—and believe, for example, that God created the earth in six actual twenty-four hour days, and that the actual age of the planet can be calculated from the genealogies in the gospels. I don't want the word "fundamentalist" to become a narrow description that excludes me, as I attend closely to the fundamentals of our faith but am most assuredly not a "fundalit.")

In any event, the woman received a phone call from her son. He had called to tell her that he had AIDS. Without hesitation, she said, "Come home." And she lovingly nursed him through his long illness until his death. According to her personal religion, that was the only thing to do, the Christian thing to do. It has, by the way, made a powerful impact on her Baptist church.

But I've also heard of families who, when they've learned that their child has AIDS, have closed the door, crying "Sin!" Statistically there is a horrifying number of people who have died of AIDS, alone, rejected by their families. Also, according to statistics, people with AIDS live in cities, but where did they come from? Where was home? It was hamlets, villages, small towns where there was no welcome. We each can ask: How ready am I to offer such hospitality? How ready is the community I live in? How prepared is my church community?

There are people who make it their life's work to care for people who, for myriad reasons, have been abandoned, turned away, disowned. Teenagers. The very old and ill. *Is* home the place where, when you have to go there, they have to take you in?

The prodigal's father didn't have to take him in, but he welcomed him with joy. Jesus' message to me in this parable is that when we come to ourselves, see ourselves as we really are, and turn with true repentance to home, God is there, waiting, loving, and welcoming us home at last. Would that we, who follow Jesus, would follow as well that loving example.

Gifts for My Girl

for my youngest daughter, Kristin

At eleven, you need new shoes
often, and I would give you
other things to stand on
that are handsome and useful
and fit you well, that are not
all plastic, that are real,
and knowable, and leather-
hard, things that will move
with you, and breathe rain
or air, and wear well
in all weather.

For beauty, I would buy
a gem from the earth's
heart and a ring that is gold
clear through, and clothes the colors
of flowers. I would cultivate in you
a gentle spirit, and curiosity,
and wonder in your eyes. For use,
in your house I'd hang
doors that are solid wood
without hidden panels of air, set
in walls built of brick more
than one inch thick.

On your floors I'd stretch fleeces
from black sheep's backs
and for your sleep, sheets
spun from fibers that grew, once,
on the flanks of the fields.
I'd mount for you one small,
clean mirror for a grinning
glimpse at yourself, and a whole
geometry of windows to the world,
with sashes that open hard, but
once lifted, let in a breath
of pure sun, the smell of a day,
a taste of wild wind, an earful
of green music.

At eleven, and always,
you will need to be nourished.
For your mind—poems and plays, words
on the pages of a thousand books:
Deuteronomy, Dante and Donne,
Hosea and Hopkins, L'Engle and Lewis.
For your spirit, mysteries and praise,
sureties and prayer. For your teeth
and tongue, real bread the color
of grain at a feast, baked and broken
fresh each day, apricots and raisins,
cheese and olive oil and honey
that live bees have brought
from the orchard. For drink
I'd pour you a wine

that remembers sun and shadow
on the hillside where it grew,
and spring water wet enough
to slake your forever thirst.

At eleven, the air around you
is full of calls and strange
directions. Choices pull at you
and a confusion of dream.
And I would show you a true compass
and how to use it, and a sun steady
in its orbit and a way
through the woods by a path
that will not peter out.

At eleven you know well
the sound of love's voice
and you have, already, hands
and a heart and a mouth
that can answer. And I
would learn with you
more of how love gives and receives,
both, with both palms open. I
am standing here, far enough away
for you to stretch and breathe,
close enough to shield you from
some of the chill and to tell you
of a comfort that is
stronger, more real,
that will come closer still.

Luci

Luci's Journal Entry

With three Johns in my life—brother, husband, son—in a moment of need, all I have to do is cry, "John!" and three men jump to help me!

Being with son John for two and a half weeks gave me a wonderful measure of the intellectual and spiritual companionship I flourish on. We drove up from San Francisco to Bellingham, camping both on the way there and the way back, talking, reading aloud, praying deeply.

While we were in Bellingham we had a family reunion (except for Jeff, whom we missed greatly). Marian and her daughter Katy flew out from Indianapolis to meet us, leaving Karl, her husband, and the other children to fend for themselves. She had not visited Bellingham before, nor seen Robin and Kris in their "home place."

My children had such a wonderful time together. Sometimes I can't believe they are the fruit of my womb, these five independent adult people. Where did the time go?—and how many times I've said that, written that here. I note it again as a theme of my journaling.

I watched like a hen brooding over her chicks, delighting as the kids found so much in common after a rather long time apart, had fun, played, told stories and jokes and also talked seriously about what is important.

The fact that I am real to them, a real person, with foibles and gifts, rather than some archetypal MOM creature, means everything to me. And they are real to me as well, not a reflection of their parents, or some part of my vision of what children should be. Real and wonderful. Thank you dear Lord for John, Jeff, Marian, Robin, Kris. Bless them. Keep them. Love them.

Friends and Lovers:

The landscape of intimacy

Come stand in my heart... and a whole river would cover your feet and rise higher and take your knees in whirlpools, and draw you down to itself, your whole body, your heart too.

—Eudora Welty

Love, as Seen from the Peanut Gallery

I think you're supposed to get shot with an arrow or something, but the rest isn't supposed to be so painful.

—Manuel, age 8

If falling in love is anything like learning to spell, I don't want to do it. It takes too long.

—Glenn, age 7

If you want to be loved by somebody who isn't in your family, it doesn't hurt to be beautiful.

—Anita, age 8

Common Ground

New dug, rail braced, young ash blond
fence posts span the frozen slope
wedlocked in pairs repeating down
the road and out of sight.
But there's an older couple
sharing the upper view across the river
(he's beech, she's thorny
bramble), whose tops feather today's
frost fog, whose ranging roots
lodge interlaced in the lean soil
that also anchors milkweed, ragweed,
thistle, sorrel, dock.

Time tangled the two (branch
and toe touched, leg locked)
season shift and shadow color them
alike, green, gold, or gray.
Rain rinses them,
westerlies bare their brows,
snows sift soft over their stiffness,
and a bleached, spring sun
speeds their slow sucking
from a common spring.

Luci

My Lover, My Friend

Madeleine

When I grew up in the younger years of this century it was expected that a young woman would marry and have children. That was her vocation. Fortunately, things have changed. Marriage is no longer the "be all and end all" for women. We don't hear the words "old maid" used any more. It was never a pleasant description. It meant failure as a woman and the closing off of the usual option, and there weren't a great many others. A single woman could be a nurse or a teacher. Bright and determined women were challenged to discover other destinies, and many did. They ran schools or hospitals, organized soup kitchens, became suffragettes. I am grateful to live at a time and place where attention is not restricted to *Kinder, Kirche,* and *Küche,* as important as all three are to me.

I didn't really expect to get married, which was not a matter of concern, as I was very serious about the vocation I did have: for all of my conscious life I had known that I am a writer. Also, I was anything but a social success. I was tall, nearsighted, and shy. Fortunately, I was also pleased with life as it was. I had good friends. I earned my living by working in the theater as an actress, happy to be general understudy or assistant stage manager, and I wrote, at every opportunity, backstage.

At age 25, I met a handsome actor named Hugh Franklin.

We went out for a hamburger and a milkshake and we talked nonstop for ten hours. When I went home I said to myself, "I have met the man I want to marry."

On a freezing cold January day while in Chicago for a run of *The Cherry Orchard*, we joined our lives in marriage and settled into living them together for what turned out to be the next forty years. I've written about these years in *Two Part Invention*.

An actor and a writer. It has only recently occurred to me that this wasn't an ordinary liaison. We were husband and wife, father and mother, lovers, friends. Sometimes we shouted. Sometimes we simply didn't communicate. Sometimes we held hands in complete intimacy. We had made promises. We made them in church, promises to each other and to God, and sometimes the promises were all that held us together. But they were good glue.

After four years we took Josephine, our first child, and left New York and the theater to have more children and to bring them up in the country. We took over and built up a run-down general store, spending the next decade in northwest Connecticut. These were difficult years for me and, in different ways, for Hugh.

I am not an instinctive housekeeper. I struggled to keep house, raised the children as best I could, questioned God and the divine purpose behind this universe and particularly this planet. I worked hard at the difficult job of a double vocation—it never occurred to me to stop writing. As full and rich as these years were, I was delighted to move back to New York, the city of my birth, the place of music and painting and theater and writing.

Sometimes at conferences or workshops I am asked about

those early years, usually by young wives, "How did you manage?" With difficulty. With conflict. With exhaustion. But I never regretted my choices, at least never for more than a few minutes.

In the later years of our marriage, after the children had grown and left home for their own lives, my husband and I had the time and space to rediscover each other. The promises still held. They had become stronger. We were friends and we were lovers. We often sat at the dinner table to eat by candlelight in a companionable silence. We were still growing interiorly, and we each gave the other room to grow.

My husband died in the fall of 1986, and not a day has passed that I have not thought of him with love and missed him terribly. I miss his body, not just in an erotic way, but his dear and known created flesh. I miss the touch of his hands as we reached out to hold each other, casually, lovingly. I miss the incredible blueness of his eyes, which were an asset to him as an actor but which were, for me, the symbol of his loving spirit.

I miss shouting at him in frustration, laughing with him in pleasure, hearing him whistle as he walked about the apartment, waiting up for him when he was working in a play. I miss our being able to grow old together. In a world where everybody is called "gentlemen," he was one.

I do believe that, ultimately, we are not separated from those we love, even in death. Hugh is bound to me still by the cords of memory. But it is more than that. In God's love, Hugh *is*, and that is all I need to know.

I'm grateful that I had a faithful marriage in a day when faithfulness is not taken as seriously as it once was. Faithfulness in marriage; faithfulness in friendship. In a world of changes and chances, fidelity is a gift and a grace. It takes time and commitment. And it is worth it.

Lovers Apart

In what, love, does fidelity consist?
I will be true to you, of course.
My body's needs I can resist,
Come back to you without remorse;

And you, behind the footlight's lure,
Kissing an actress on the stage,
Will leave her presence there, I'm sure,
As I my people on the page.

And yet—I love you, darling, yet
I sat with someone at a table
And gloried in our minds that met
As sometimes strangers' minds are able

To leap the bounds of times and spaces
And find, in sharing wine and bread
And light in one another's faces
And in the words that each has said

An intercourse so intimate
It shook me deeply, to the core.
I said good-night, for it was late;
We parted at my hotel door

And I went in, turned down the bed
And took my bath and thought of you
Leaving the theatre with light tread
And going off, as you should do,

To rest, relax, and eat and talk—
And I lie there and wonder who
Will wander with you as you walk
And what you both will say and do...

We may not love in emptiness;
We married in a peopled place;
The vows we made enrich and bless
The smile on every stranger's face,

And all the years that we have spent
Give me the joy that makes me able
To love and laugh with sacrament
Across a strange and distant table.

No matter where I am, you are,
We two are one and bread is broken
And laughter shared both near and far
Deepens the promises once spoken

And strengthens our fidelity
Although I cannot tell you how,
But I rejoice in mystery
And rest upon our marriage vow.

Madeleine

Prothalamion

How like an arch our marriage! Framed
in living stone, its gothic arrow aimed
at heaven, with Christ (its Capstone and
its Arrowhead) locking our coupled
weakness into one, the leaning
of two lives into a strength.
Thus he defines our joining's length
and width, its archetypal shape. Its meaning
is another thing: a letting in of light,
an opening to a varied landscape, planned
but yet to be explored. A paradox, for you
and I, who doubly frame this arch, may now step through
its entrance into the promised land.

Luci

When Two Become One, Rejoice!

Luci

When special people in my life get married I sometimes write a wedding poem as a gift, and my friend Timothy Botts, the skilled calligrapher, before he became famous and busy, would inscribe them for me to frame. One of these was a wedding poem for Robin, my eldest daughter, when she and Mark were married by a small lake in an Illinois forest preserve. One of the lines mentioned "loud frog-song" as part of the rejoicing of the creatures, human and wild, at this happy event in its natural woodland setting. I read the poem aloud as part of Robin and Mark's wedding ceremony, and at the very moment I read the line about the frogs, a deep, booming croak, followed by a softer, treble croak, sounded from the lily pads by the water's edge. Madeleine was a guest at the wedding, and she asked me later, incredulous, "How did you manage that?"

"Only by the grace of God," I answered, smiling mysteriously.

My son John was married last year, at the age of thirty-six, in Switzerland, to Christa Fluri. John, who for years had a series of attractive girlfriends, finally found the woman God planned for him. The wait had been long and frustrating, but now the wait is forgotten, as they forge a new life together. The wedding poem I wrote for him, "Possess your soul in patience," was written out of my own joy at their joy, and I read it aloud as part of the wedding sermon I preached, by translation, in the little church in Wallisellen, near Zurich. When Jeff and Kristin find their future spouses, I hope a poem will rise to the top of my mind, like cream, to celebrate my delight and contentment with their marriages.

Possess your soul in patience
Wedding poem for John and Christa

Own it. Hold your heart the way
you'd hold a live bird—your two hands
laced to latch it in, feeling
its feathery trembling, its fledgling
warmth, its faint anxieties
of protest, its heart stutter
against the palm of one hand, a fidget
in the pull of early light.

Possess it, restless, in
the finger cage of patience. Enfold
this promise with a blue sheen
on its neck, its wings a tremor
of small feathered bones
until morning widens like
a window, and God opens
your fingers and whispers, *Fly!*

Luci

A continuing conversation

MADELEINE: When I'm with you or my other married women friends I sometimes feel a sense of partialness. It isn't just loneliness. It's a lack of completion.

LUCI: You think a woman *has* to have a man?

MADELEINE: No. No, I think I'm too much of a feminist for that. I think it's that having had the fulfillment of a lifetime commitment to someone with whom I had many varieties of friendship—sex, companionship, play, excitement, support—and knowing how good it can be, I miss it, particularly when I'm with a large group of people, many of whom are couples.

LUCI: But there are marriages that don't supply those elements—that aren't very good.

MADELEINE: That's another story. Some marriages are obviously better than others. Some need work and can benefit from it, while others probably aren't ever going to make it.

LUCI: "Work" is certainly the operative word here. I guess the two of us have some wisdom from our combined years of marriage that would allow us to say that marriage is a lot of work! I know there is a feeling out there, in the culture, that you are supposed to feel happy and fulfilled in your marriage automatically, almost as if that went with the ring and the ceremony. That is certainly not how it is. It leaves out the idea that you need to have decided that this relationship is valuable and you are going to invest time and energy in it, even when that is very difficult.

MADELEINE: Yes, and don't we both know people who have just said that they are not "happy" in their marriage so they are going to end it, and look elsewhere for "happiness," which can lead you on quite a chase.

LUCI: Of course, happiness *is* a part of marriage, although I think I might say that "contentment" describes it better, especially as years wear on. My marriages have been filled with joy, and some pain, and hard work. There is nothing superficial about all this!

MADELEINE: I have also seen marriages that had to end, that should end, where there is nothing creative anymore, nothing that reflects health or love.

LUCI: Yes, and I have had friends who have struggled with this, and then made the difficult decision to end the marriage. You can't really talk about this in absolutes.

MADELEINE: Not long ago, I was talking with a woman whose husband had died just before Hugh, and she said, "The first year I'd have married anyone who asked me. Now I like living alone, and doing my own thing, and the last thing in the world I want is another husband."

LUCI: That's how I felt before I married John Hoyte. Really happy, fulfilled, enriched in myself with God, all on my own. But romance bloomed when he showed up on our blind date! A real surprise, followed by a very impetuous engagement! How do you feel now, about remarriage?

MADELEINE: I think I've reached an age where finding someone I'd want to marry just isn't very likely. Sometimes I'll enjoy being with someone, and then I'll ask myself: "Would you like to have breakfast with this person every single morning, before he's shaved and had his shower?" And I haven't answered yes to that one yet. But, you know me, Luci. Never say never.

Spice

Sentimentalists, purists, and some
preachers, advocate marital absolutes—
stability, a clear hierarchy for
decision, a predictable union, unflawed,
bland as a blank page. No wonder
it ends up flat. A truer wedding's
grounded in paradox, answers the pull
of the particular, grapples a score
of rugged issues. Like horned toads
in Eden, incongruities add surprise
to a complacent landscape.

Thank heaven you're romantic and
irascible, I'm opinionated in my
impulsiveness. Thank God we can
lean together in our failing—a rusty
trellis propping a thorned rose.

Luci

Feasts of Friendship:

Love revealed

The Ministry of Tomato Soup

Madeleine

Friends give nourishment of all kinds to one another. We *sustain* one another—provide *sustenance*. In so many ways we offer to one another the feasts of our friendship.

When Hugh and I and our children lived in the village where the old colonial church was the center of our lives, my special church friends and I brought food to our neighbors, especially if someone was ill and the household thereby out of kilter. We carried in soups, stews, or maybe a ham, and we looked around the house and, if necessary, did some quick cleaning, washed dishes, ironed a shirt that had been left on the board. Providing nourishment in this way was part of how we understood Christian community.

It has certainly been the custom in any community I have ever been part of for friends and neighbors to bring in food in vast quantities after a death. This is both a comfort and an affirmation of life despite the inevitability of death.

Often, after a funeral and the sharing of grief, Hugh and I would go home, sit at our little table and enjoy a simple meal, and then we would make love. This was no dishonor to the person who had just been buried, but an affirmation of life. Perhaps it harkens back to primordial times when the planet was very sparsely populated. Death and birth were very precariously balanced and the mandate to "replenish the earth" made sense; procreation meant the preservation of the species.

A shared meal brings a special comfort in times of sadness. The summer Hugh was dying we ate out on the terrace every night, and God laid on the most incredible sunsets. A feast for the eyes. There have been very few as splendid since. We'd sit there while the stars came out. And there was something unspokenly sacramental about it that was strengthening, and still is, for me.

In my view, eating outdoors adds a festive air, whatever the circumstances. The Europeans have always understood this, and we're catching on, with outdoor restaurants springing up everywhere, even on the sidewalks of New York. Sitting outside together for a meal, watching people strolling by, couples holding hands, allows us to bask, not just in the sun, but in our companionship, our camaraderie.

Companion. Comrade. Both good words. A good comrade gives comfort.

When Luci and I talked about this, she added that a good comrade also gives you comfort food. The night she and John decided to get married, right after his proposal they made tea and buttered toast with Marmite. "Buttered toast is homey and comforting," she said. I nodded, adding "Cream of tomato soup."

"Oh, yes," Luci said, "my favorite, too."

And isn't it wondrous: a simple bowl of tomato soup with buttered toast can be a feast of friendship.

With Love in Every Stitch

Luci

In my childhood, our family often took a birthday picnic lunch to the beach or the bush or a park in whatever country we happened to be living at the time—England, Australia, or Canada. My mother planned lovely picnics. There were always hardboiled eggs, and crisp lettuce leaves, and cold fried chicken, and parsley-and-Marmite sandwiches, and cheese scones with butter, and egg-and-bacon pie (we'd call it quiche today), and pikelets—small New Zealand pancakes, served cold, with butter and honey—and lemonade, and fruit salad. And then we'd all lie in the sun-bright grass and read some favorite book aloud, and sing hymns.

Another birthday tradition passed down from my parents is a family reading of Psalm 103, so richly full of God's promises and blessings. A birthday tradition I've developed with my own children is the baking of my famous hot-milk sponge cake, which is delicious without being too rich. It has a festive design made by sifting powdered sugar over a lace paper doily on the cake's top layer, and then removing the doily. The filling is always a mix of whipped cream and crushed raspberries, or strawberries, or peaches, according to the wishes of the birthday person.

Within the family, books were often the gifts of choice, and still are. I just sent my two sons books—to Jeff in London and John in South Africa; their natal days are only five days apart.

Of course, when my children were in the start-up phase in their independent lives, beginning to support themselves in their first jobs, money gifts were always welcome, or some household item—a toaster, a blanket, a set of glasses—for their first apartment.

I've often knitted sweaters as special gifts—birthday, Christmas, or "just because I love you" gifts. I've lost count of the number of sweaters I've knitted, but the total's probably close to four hundred. Madeleine got one about fifteen years ago, and when she began to pester me for another, I told her I'd add her to my waiting list. "But I want to be at the top of the list" she complained. "Sorry, you'll have to wait your turn! Fair is fair."

Of course, sweaters as gifts require serious pre-planning months before the birthday in question. For many years I developed my own variations on an Aran Fisherman theme, intricately patterned, using the wonderful, cream-colored yarn called "bainin" with the sheep's lanolin still in it, which makes the garment naturally waterproof. But lately I've branched out to other styles and yarns. On a visit to a knitting mill in Wales I bought yarn from the Bargain Bin, woolen thread in discontinued but charming shades, wound on the cone-shaped spindles used on the knitting machines. As I remember, they were an incredible buy at thirty-five pence per spindle, and each spindle held a sweater's worth of yarn, which translates to less than two dollars a sweater. I was enchanted by the subtle, heathery shades of blues and greens lying higgledy-piggledy in the sale bin, and I loaded up for future knitting. Now son John has a crew-neck sweater in mossy green with all-over chevrons to lend him warmth in the chilly South African winters. And I'm finally finishing Madeleine's garment—a two-tone cardigan with pewter buttons, knit in a slate-teal blue with gray. I've promised this to her when our current writing project—the book you hold in your hand—is finally completed. Perhaps as you read it, Madeleine will be wearing her sweater!

When my grandchildren began to arrive I got to work knitting baby blankets, booties, sweaters for early birthdays—a nice change from the very utilitarian clothes I sewed when my own babies came, when we were too poor for store-bought clothes. Birthday gifts in those days were mere tokens of love, and had to be useful rather than beautiful.

I found a wonderful gift card in a gift shop. It shows a mother sheep at work with her knitting needles, fashioning a sweater from a strand of yarn drawn from the wool on her own sheeply body (which leaves her looking a little naked). I bought enough copies of this card to last me for years of sweater giving because I feel like that sheep: knitting means giving a part of myself. And since creative knitting is one of the joys of my life when I do it for people dear to me (I even knit in board meetings; it helps me focus), I write on these gift cards, "Every stitch is knit with love." And it's true.

Luci's Hot Milk Sponge Cake

Set oven to 325 degrees.

IN A MIXING BOWL:

Beat 4 eggs well, using electric mixer on high speed.
Gradually beat in 2 c. sugar, 2 t. vanilla.
Beat together until light.

IN SEPARATE BOWL:

Combine 2 c. flour, 2 t. baking powder, 1/2 t. salt.
Fold into egg mixture.

IN SMALL PAN:

Bring to boil 1 c. milk and 2 t. butter or margarine.

Add milk mixture slowly to batter, stirring gently.
Pour into two well-greased and floured 8" cake pans.
Bake 30-35 minutes.

When cool, frost one layer with whipped cream and jam (I use raspberry or strawberry) or crushed fresh fruit and top with the second layer.

Lay a paper lace doily on top and sift powdered sugar over the cake. Remove doily. *Voilà!* A cake for a festive occasion.

Let Us Break Bread Together

Madeleine

The word "companion" has its derivation from the words "bread" and "with." A companion is someone you break bread with. In my life the breaking of bread at the evening meal can be the most important time of the day. It is the time to gather around the table, light the candles—in candlesticks Luci so beautifully polishes—ask the blessing, and eat and talk together. Having friends for dinner is a great joy. Sometimes these dinners are planned ahead, often they occur spontaneously, sometimes unexpectedly.

New York is a crossroads and a departure place for other destinations. The phone will ring and I'll hear an excited voice: "I'm off to London (or Cairo, or Buenos Aires, or Cape Town) and I'm here overnight. Any chance we can get together?"

"Wonderful! Can you come for dinner?"

"Oh, I'd love to, but I have a couple of people with me—you'd really like them. Would it be too much trouble? Could we order in Chinese food or something?"

"Don't worry. Just come. It will be marvelous to see you."

My favorite "quick-and-easy-yet-elegant" meal is leg of lamb. I call my wonderful butcher, get a large bag of new potatoes to cook along with the lamb, and plan to make creamed spinach, which is easy to do with low-fat cream cheese, garlic, and nutmeg. Preparing the lamb is simple. I sliver large quantities of garlic and poke it into little slits made with a sharp knife all over the lamb, then rub the lamb with rosemary and mustard. The new potatoes are placed in the roasting pan with the lamb, and it goes into a 350 degree oven for two hours. Dessert will be fruit and cheese. A wonderful dinner, with little effort.

Setting the table takes about the same time as preparing the meal. If Luci is with me she will insist on ironing the napkins! I fill the big silver pitcher with ice water. It is rather ornate and was given to my mother as a wedding present. She didn't like ornate things, so as soon as I was married she gave it to me, and I love it, and use it all the time.

A blessing of living in an old apartment, built in 1912, is that I have an actual dining room, and an oval table which comfortably seats eight, though we've squeezed in twelve. There's a view across the Hudson River to New Jersey, and we're on the route of many planes. They streak across the sky like stars.

Around the table we are one, though often we are a disparate group. Paul grew up in Colombia, working in a Roman Catholic hospital. Patty is from a Baptist family in Georgia, and her work has been with abused teenagers. Somehow the circle of grace at the table, the food shared, the ideas tossed out with eagerness and hope, bridge the differences. Our ideas for healing may be strangely different, but the ultimate aim is the same. We try to listen.

We sit around the table and sing one of the graces we know, an old round. The candles are lit. We break into a crusty loaf of bread. I pass the salad: mixed greens and nuts in a simple dressing of olive oil, balsamic vinegar, salt and pepper, a tiny amount of prepared dark mustard, and more garlic, with goat cheese, lots of goat cheese, on top.

When I was a little girl in France, only the peasants ate goat cheese. That has changed, too, and it has implications beyond what it is or is not fashionable to eat. We live now in a wider world. We try new tastes. We listen to new ideas. We sometimes feel threatened, but we try to be open and to discover whether the threat comes from within ourselves, or is really something from without.

We talk and talk, catching up with what has gone on in our lives, in the world around us. There is always a crisis somewhere on the planet. There's an ongoing crisis in the daily lives of many of us. Many of my friends worry about the state of the church which we love and which we know is in danger of being trapped in its institutional forms. As life changes, so must our understanding of what it means to be a human being loved by and loving our Creator. This is no time for separation, for dividing into denominations and sects and *us* and *them*. We know that the planet, indeed, the whole universe, is a living organism, and what happens to any part of it affects all. Nobody, nothing is left out. The time for criticism and condemnation without mercy and compassion is over. What are we to do? What is that Edwin Markham poem I learned in high school?...

> *He drew a circle that shut me out—*
> *Heretic, rebel, a thing to flout.*
> *But Love and I had the wit to win:*
> *We drew a circle that took him in.*

Around the table we sit, as the candles flicker and burn down. We share ideas. We share food. We share our sense of calling, affirming again that we are here to do God's will and praying we will be given the grace to discern what God's will is.

Love. Inclusion. Compassion. Openness. Willingness to listen to new ideas, to change. Lamb and potatoes. Bread and wine. Enjoyed together, in the understanding that all of life is a sacrament. We are companions.

Pilgrim Bread

(from the kitchen of Marian, Luci's second daughter)

MIX IN A BOWL:

    1/2 c. white or yellow corn meal
    1/3 c. brown sugar
    1 T. salt

STIR IN GRADUALLY:

    2 c. boiling water

ADD:

    1/4 c. oil, and cool to lukewarm.

DISSOLVE:

    2 packages of dry yeast in 1/2 c. warm water.
    Add yeast to corn meal mixture.

BEAT IN:

    3/4 c. + 1/2 c. whole wheat flour.

Turn onto lightly floured surface. Knead until smooth and elastic. Place in greased bowl, turning once to grease surface. Cover and let rise until doubled.

Punch down. Turn onto lightly floured surface and divide in half.

Knead again for 3 minutes. Shape into two loaves and place in greased bread pans.

Cover, and let rise until double. Bake at 375 degrees for 45 minutes.

Garlic and Other Delights

Madeleine

Have you ever OD'ed on garlic? It can be a revelatory experience. Luci and I baked two whole buds of garlic, took a loaf of French bread, a bottle of white wine, and settled down to a quiet evening of conversation. We each ate our whole bud of garlic, every clove, and half a loaf of bread and solved the problems of the world and the church and most of our friends and went happily to bed.

In the morning I asked quietly, "Luci, did you have fierce gas last night?"

She nodded.

It was worth it.

A recipe less likely to blow you up came from my godson, Terry Moore, on Orcas Island. In a little olive oil cook up some onions and garlic. Then add black olives and green olives, artichoke hearts, a cup or so of cherry tomatoes, depending on how many people are eating, and, at the last minute so they retain their freshness, put in circles of red, green and yellow peppers. Serve over pasta. You won't have much left.

After I'd had my first dish of this on Orcas, we went down to the beach, five of us, and read Evening Prayer and Compline in the twilight, taking turns with the psalm verses, one, two, three, four, five.

When Luci and Bara and I travel together we enjoy feasts

for soul and body. On a wonderful trip to Scotland we discovered, after a first tentative taste, that haggis is delicious. We ate full Scottish breakfasts, and skipped lunch. We keep talking about taking time occasionally to make a Scottish breakfast, but the pace of New York has not allowed it, and this is not good.

My habit in the winter is to made a big batch of Irish oatmeal, add golden raisins and some flax seed, and put it in half a dozen small dishes in the fridge. Then, each morning I just warm one bowlful a couple of minutes in the microwave, splash some buttermilk on top, and begin my day happily fortified.

Sometimes, if Bara and I are late at meetings, our dinner will be a slice of paté, some cornichons, a mixed green salad with goat cheese and a loaf of crusty bread. Sometimes we want comfort food—meat loaf and garlic-mashed potatoes and creamed spinach. My recipe for meatloaf comes from the oatmeal box, with imaginative additions and substitutions. Thus fed, we prepare for Compline and give thanks for this feast, and the feasts of life, and friendship.

Of Bread and Bacon

Luci

When Madeleine, Bara, and I were traveling the British Isles, sometimes we splurged a bit, staying in some elegant old manor houses that had been turned into hotels, all of them with extensive grounds and the most *haute* of *haute cuisine*. But whether we were lodged in splendor or housed in a homely B & B, we relished the cooked breakfasts—haggis, kippers, fried tomatoes and eggs, and *especially* fried bread!

I remember how my mother, a superb cook, would make fried bread with a mere scrape of bacon fat. Yet it would come to the breakfast table crisply brown and deliciously bacon-y, without any excess greasiness. American "fry bread" doesn't quite approximate it. The making of proper fried bread is an essentially British skill. And my mother, born in the 19th century in New Zealand, was almost obsessively British.

Simple Pleasures

Madeleine

One of my happy memories from the days when our children were little is summer evenings when family and friends gathered for the sparkler parade. Even the toddlers could hold a sparkler with moderate safety, and the grownups would watch the children, led by the older ones, dance in and out of the fruit trees in the orchard.

This past July we had our picnic with another generation of children. I had been sent a large box of sparklers from Texas, and the children, four little boys, waited for dark and then ran around the field making great sweeping patterns with their sparklers, and it was beautiful.

There was a special poignancy for me in watching the faces of the parents who had, a couple of decades ago, been part of the sparkler parade, now looking with love at their own children making patterns of light.

Life is full of such small moments, simple pleasures. Each year I cultivate a greater appreciation of such simple feasts. In their own way, they are as satisfying as sumptuous banquets.

Days of Fasting:

Solitude and loneliness

A friend is that other person with whom we can share our solitude, our silence, and our prayer. A friend is that other person with whom we can look at a tree and say, "Isn't that beautiful," or sit on the beach and silently watch the sun disappear under the horizon. With a friend we don't have to say or do something special. With a friend we can be still and know that God is there with both of us.

Henri Nouwen
Bread for the Journey

Madeleine

Solitude and loneliness—though outwardly they may look the same—come from different kinds of fasting. Solitude is the chosen fast, while loneliness is the unbidden hunger. Solitude brings a deeper kind of living. Loneliness brings a kind of death.

One reason *Emily of New Moon* was my favorite book when I was a child was that Emily understood that the test of real friendship is mutual solitude: being together, and yet being able to be silent, with no need to chatter. Some people need to fill any silence with some kind of talk, and even their talking has to be filled with what is called an articulated pause: *you know, er, um,* etc. For forty years I had the blessing of a husband with whom I could be silent; we enjoyed our mutual solitude.

It's an odd thing that the people with whom I can have the most comfortable solitude can also cause the greatest loneliness and anxiety. I suppose that is because we are most sensitive to the feelings of those we love most, and share in what they feel.

I love my chosen solitudes, time to relax, usually in silence, occasionally with music. When my children were young I sometimes took a long subway ride downtown to a friend's apartment. We would play piano duets for an hour, and then I would have a relatively peaceful subway ride home, about ten o'clock. There was little time in those days for loneliness.

Now for me, as for many women who are alone, there is more opportunity for solitude, but also more time for loneliness. When I am being solitary, I am comfortable within myself, and not anxious. When I am lonely I am often anxious, worried.

I try to alleviate anxiety with prayer, because anxiety is seldom helpful. I try to pray quietly, to put whatever the problem is into God's loving hands. But God never promised us security, or that everything—in temporal terms—will be all right. There are accidents, mortal illnesses, and while I know that in God's time, *kairos*, all indeed will be all right, in *chronos*, in which we live, we have fears, losses. Loneliness.

I try to turn the loneliness of occasional insomnia into solitude, but I am not always successful, because my body needs sleep, especially if I have a heavy schedule ahead of me. These middle of the night solitudes are not chosen, so they are not always successful.

Silence isn't necessary for solitude, but it's a help. Those of us who live in cities—and there are more and more of us—have very little real silence. In New York, where I live for much of the year, the only silent time is somewhere between two and four in the morning. When I am in the country, my bedroom faces a sweep of field, woods, and a mountain, and there is silence, real silence.

Sometimes when sleep eludes me and outside noises intrude, I will turn on the light and read, and find my solitude in a book. I love being with the characters of a good novel, but sometimes they are *too* engaging, so I pick up a book of theology or philosophy by an academic writer who uses an excessive number of footnotes and a plethora of words and bore myself to sleep. This is not solitude!

The three sons of one of my friends grew up all sleeping in the same room. When the youngest found himself there alone, with his older brothers off in college, he complained that he could not sleep because he needed to hear people breathing. I understand that! It was easier to be wakeful in the small hours of the morning when I could hear my husband's peaceful breathing beside me.

Touch can bring the sense of shared solitude in times of grief or great stress. Sitting and holding hands while waiting for a telephone call, or outside a hospital room, can give us relief. Once as I waited in the waiting room while my mother was having surgery, I found companionship with the parents of a young girl, also in surgery. Most of the time we simply sat in silence together, sharing a solitude of concern and love. It was in most ways not a chosen solitude, until we were able to reach out to each other, no longer strangers.

We can be lonely in strange and unexpected places. I have been lonely in church, surrounded by people I care about, sharing in worship, and yet assailed by a great, cosmic loneliness. This is part of the human predicament. It is not helped by coffee hour! Garrulousness does not help. It just covers up a loneliness which needs to be faced. What we usually need is a caring person who has experienced this same loneliness and understands.

In a strange way, moving through the fast of loneliness can prepare us for the particular richness of solitude. When we have moved through the death of loneliness, we are ready for the deeper life of solitude.

The soul unto itself
Is an imperial friend—
Or the most agonizing spy
An enemy could send.

         —Emily Dickinson

I have three entire days alone—three
pure and rounded pearls.

         —Virginia Woolf

The Balancing Act

Luci

It often seems my life consists in balancing between two extremes, and never quite coming out even. Being with like minds is energizing. For a while, it fills me with pinging exhilaration, but I reach a point when I know I'm running on adrenaline. I admit I'm quite addicted to my own adrenaline. I love the stimulation of new thoughts, new experiences, and the challenge of charging into a strenuous task, completing it successfully, and feeling the warm pulse of gratification.

But after days or weeks of living at this pitch, I begin to feel the rawness of over-worked emotions and I know that I am about to crash. I feel a physical hunger to be alone, to have time for me, to allow long nights of sleep to wash over me, and days of relaxation to slow my rhythms. Most of all, because in times of great productivity and busy-ness my prayers tend to be the brief arrow prayers that yell for help and strength, I know I need to be still enough to hear God's whispered voice in my inner heart again, and enter into a long, serene conversation.

The best medicine in this particular circumstance for me is to get away, alone in my little car, and drive to the mountains or some coastal shore with a remote campground. With my cozy dome tent and sleeping bag I can escape civilization and the babble of competing voices and demands, and pay attention to the wild, wonderful, universal messages of the stars and the clouds, as well as the textures and shades of the individual stones and waves and fronds of moss and ferns that swim into my view. All of them are voices from my Creator, and of the Creation of which I am a part. Much of the time I'll nap and read, nap and read (old journals, or a good novel), and pray, and sing, unselfconscious, at the top of my voice. I stretch my legs with long walks and open my eyes wide to peer at the patterns of the wild through my camera.

Slowly my spiritual and emotional batteries recharge. Time and quiet do their healing work and I read the book of nature—as vital to me as my Bible and with the same truth-telling author. And as we converse, listening to each other in the silence of solitude, my soul is led gently back to healing and wholeness. I am ready to pack up my tent, and return to another life, another pace.

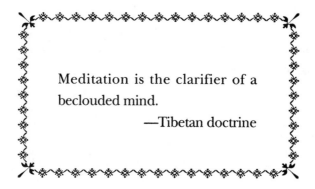

Meditation is the clarifier of a beclouded mind.
                —Tibetan doctrine

The Birth of Love

To learn to love
is to be stripped of all love
until you are wholly without love
because
until you have gone
naked and afraid
into this cold dark place
where all love is taken from you
you will not know
that you are wholly within love.

Madeleine

Luci's Journal Entry

As I grow older I seem to experience more prolonged periods of the silence of God. George MacDonald talks about this pattern in The Wise Woman. *It feels like winter in the heart—a season when I long for the warmth and growth of springtime for my soul, but the trees are bare skeletons, and the fields are flattened by heavy ice and snow. It's deprivation, a starvation diet, as when friends are out of touch or out of reach for reasons beyond my control.*

But this is where faith comes into play—a hanging on to the truth that the friend is there, that God is there for me, with me, whether or not I feel God's life-giving presence. I know that if my days were routinely sun-filled and exciting, if my prayers always received obvious and immediate answers, if expectations were automatically fulfilled, there would be no need for me to have faith. I have come to understand faith as a heart-muscle that needs to be exercised diligently if it is to grow strong.

I believe God trusts me to continue to trust even when I don't see or feel or hear from him. I may wish for nonstop epiphanies, but God, in divine wisdom, gives me just enough sightings to keep me going year after year in the knowledge that he loves me, and that someday I'll be face-to-face, eye-to-eye with him, knowing him as completely as he now knows me.

Faith in a friend's love is the anchor that gives me confidence in times of separation. Faith in my God, and the continued hunger for him, is the magnet that keeps pulling me forward toward heaven, without giving up.

Hello and Then Good-Bye:

The rhythm of presence

Circles and Cycles

Madeleine

We live in cycles and move in circles. We meet, and then part. Hello and good-bye. That is the way of the world, or at least as I have experienced it. As we care about friendship, we need to note and mark these comings and goings, and nurture one another through the temporary separations along the way to the profoundly different separation that comes in death.

With all of our absences from our friends, how we keep in touch becomes a matter of great importance, a matter about which we must be intentional if we are to maintain and nurture our friends and our friendships.

Years ago a friend said to me, "After forty it's maintenance, maintenance, maintenance." I'm approaching double that, and it's true. The idea that one needs less sleep as one ages is absurd. I need more. My joints creak. Has the original lubrication just leaked away over the years? Undoubtedly by now I have shrunk a little, but I'm still around 5'10". One thing I will never be is a *little* old lady.)

As we do what we can to maintain our bodies, so we must do with our friendships. How many deep friendships can one maintain? This is different for different people, depending on temperament and many other factors, inner and outer. I think we each have some understanding about this, even if we haven't given it a great deal of conscious thought. Too many deep friendships can put us on overload; friendship would (and sometimes does) drift back into acquaintanceship, or even forgetfulness. Though I have no idea of the number, I am amazed and awed by the people who are my friends, and who care about maintaining our friendship.

Old friends are a particular treasure, especially as we grow older and the friendships stretch over half a century. I met Cavada when we were beginning our teens; we were in boarding school together for four years, then college, then several years living near each other in Greenwich Village. Then geography, as so often happens, separated us. Cavada lives in London and sometimes we don't see each other for years, and letters are sporadic. Occasionally the phone will ring and I'll answer it and hear that dear familiar voice that seems to have changed little. When I'm in London, which is once every few years, we immediately get together, and it is as though no time had passed, and we are as close as we were in school when our rooms were just a few doors apart. Somehow the fact that we have known each other "forever" makes the friendship easier to maintain. It simply *is*.

I met Marilyn at that same conference in Wheaton where I met Luci, and our conversation was immediately deep and probing, reaching out to God's unequivocal love.

Throughout the years how often Marilyn has rescued me in time of crisis, bringing me home from the hospital after surgery, traveling with me when my speaking commitments took me across the continent in a wheelchair, which she learned to toss like a discus into her van. Marilyn's loving and competent care has been prayer in action, and when we have been able to be together just for fun, it has been fun indeed.

Despite the shock of the bill each month, the telephone is a blessing. I met the retired archbishop, David Somerville, and his wife, Fran, in Vancouver about ten years ago, and we are a continent apart most of the year. When I am offered a speaking job anywhere near Vancouver I accept it! But most of the time it is the phone that keeps us together, and we *are* together because of our common commitment to our friendship and our shared interests. We have the same passion for literature, music, theology. We are awed, rather than distressed, by the discoveries about our amazing universe which may, indeed, be one of many universes. How can God keep track of it all? What kind of a God do we believe in? Conversations begun in person continue on the phone, and it is important for me to know that, thanks to telephonic marvels, we can be in touch within seconds.

Telephone calls are also a lifeline to Pat, whom I have known almost as long as I have known Cavada. Pat lives in Florida and we manage to see each other at least once a year. Between times, our phone calls are as long as though we were still teenagers. There's always something to talk about: our kids, grandkids, the work it takes for a single woman to keep in the midst of things in a society based on couples, her retirement ("Retirement!" I exclaim. "What retirement?") She was a physician, the chief public health officer of a large city, and is still on a dozen boards.

She sends me articles from medical journals, and one by Lewis Thomas in *The New England Journal of Medicine* radically changed and undergirded one of my fantasies, books which are based on post-Newtonian physics.

I credit Betty Anne for being forthright with me many years ago about the demands of friendship. When it became apparent that our acquaintanceship was growing into a deep friendship, she wrote me a long letter about the maintenance of friendship, particularly when the friends are mostly apart.

She lives in San Antonio, Texas, so we see each other only by special planning. On her list she included frequent letters and phone calls. Keeping in touch. Not letting too much time slide by without checking up on each other. We've worked at it, and I am grateful to her for her intentionality, as she is to me.

How long have Bara and I known each other? A dozen years. It has been a joy to watch our friendship deepen, ripen, become vulnerable and intimate. We were remarking today that the more people we love the more vulnerable we are. We have shared in our blood and guts, our children's pains and disappointments, and their joys, too. Sometimes when we read Compline together in the evening it will take us an hour or more, because we will interrupt this ancient office with thoughts it has awakened. This shared vulnerability, turned over to God, in itself strengthens our friendship. And then, of course, we do laugh a lot. I don't think I could reveal my deepest self to anyone who wasn't able to laugh outrageously at something that strikes us both as funny.

In all of these friendships there is mutuality: a mutual knowing that the other is to be counted on, in spite of how often we see one another, in spite of all of our hellos and good-byes. Our friendships have been tested over the years in a variety of ways and the testing has made them stronger.

How often have I said that friendship, for me, keeps the stars in their courses? Not only that: could I keep on believing in a loving God if I had no friends? I am not sure. My friends are God-bearers for me, as I am called to be for them.

Good-bye is no longer spelled as I am spelling it here, using the spelling that was still standard until a few years ago: *good-bye*, short for *God be with you.* In the new spelling it is easy to forget the original meaning. *God be with you* is a prayer in parting and a promise that we will remain in one another's prayers.

I'll be with you in spirit! we say to our friends sometimes when we can't be together. Letters, phone calls, visits, sharing and laughing together, the "being there" for one another at times when it really counts—all of these are vital to the maintenance of our friendships. However, at the heart of it all is the "spirit connection" that comes with prayer. When we pray for our friends we join our lives with theirs in a way that is as profound as it is mysterious. May it always be so.

✧

The separation

No matter how intense our touching,
or how tender—fingers sure, or silken—
there are no contiguous nerves
to bridge our bodies' gaps, no
paths of words to join our souls.
Though each images the other's pain or
pleasure, two remain two.
We have been seamed, not grafted.
Though our steps interlock,
each dances his own dance.
Do you read into this a strategy:
separation for survival's sake?
See it rather as predicament—
our world's ache to be joined,
to know or be known.

Luci

We lay aside letters never to read them again, and at last destroy them out of discretion, and so disappears the most beautiful, the most immediate breath of life, irrecoverably for ourselves and for others.

—Goethe

Adjustments and Accommodations

Luci

When John Hoyte married me, he thought he knew what he was getting into—a wife who was booked two to three years ahead with workshops, lectures, retreats, readings. In actual fact, I think John has had to get used to lots more hellos and good-byes than he had bargained for. I am blessed that he has made this adjustment with great grace. Fortunately, he's an easygoing, energetic guy who is willing to drop me off at airports at ungodly hours in the morning and pick me up late at night. Even more important, he has never made me feel guilty for being away so much.

And I have had my own adjustments to make to his schedule. He is an engineer and his company designs and manufactures analytical instruments to test air and water purity. He also travels widely, attending environmental conferences around the continent and making new business contacts abroad. I thought I had a high energy level until I met John, who gets up at 6:00 A.M. and rarely falls asleep until midnight, moving faster, the rest of the time, than the proverbial speeding bullet.

If our experience is at all typical, a marriage of two traveling spouses requires ongoing planning, juggling schedules and logistics, and the reluctant acceptance of the times of being apart. Conversations begun in the morning continue on the phone in the evening, or sometimes just dangle off. Issues, even important ones, get raised and then can too easily be put on hold if you aren't careful. Under these circumstances, the relationship needs a tailor-made kind of nurturing, something each couple must work out for themselves with great intention. In our case, it is important that we stay in daily touch while we're on the road, with phone calls every night and now, e-mail. Equally, we plan stretches of time together, for each other, perhaps camping or traveling or just at home.

John and I already anticipate days of greater leisure when we can travel more *together*, as we did last year to New Zealand. This will mean, blessedly, more hellos to new places and fewer good-byes to each other. Until that day comes, we are committed to giving the rhythm of our relationship the special attention it needs, and deserves.

The Final Good-Bye—And Yet, Not

Madeleine

I took my beloved aunt, well up in her eighties, to the hospital to die. *Oh good-bye, dear Aunt. God be with you on this last journey.* A few years earlier I had said my final good-bye to my father as he put me on the train to go to boarding school, and I somehow knew that I would not see him alive again.

How do we keep in touch with those who have moved on to the larger life? Memory is good, but not enough. We have lost much of our native awareness of the spirit world, and our sense of the permanence of our spirits, our *selves.* This was formerly a matter of great importance for the entire community. I am not speaking of contrived séances and trances, but rather a communal sense of the "blessed company of all faithful people," and of the "communion of saints." Through our prayer for those to whom we have said a final earthly good-bye, we strengthen our connection with them and their world, which is to be our own home when we end our earthly sojourn.

It seems to me that the church (of all denominations) has somehow not put forward a valid theology of resurrection, and not really moved past medieval ideas of heaven and hell. Heaven, for example, sounds excruciatingly dull, and I do not believe God is ever dull.

The church does tend to make definitions, and then announce them to believers. We used to be told that Christians could not be cremated, because God is not capable of doing anything with ashes. What kind of a puny, ineffective god is that? The church also put into literal terms the poetry of death and resurrection and the last trump. For centuries we were taught to believe that our very bodies, exactly as they were when they were put into the grave, would rise again at the last day. It would not please my grandfather, who died when he was 101 years old, to be resurrected in that ancient body.

We do not know what resurrection means, and when we try for simple definitions, we lose it; the glory slips away in inadequate explanations.

I do not know what the husband I lost to death is doing, or where he is doing it. And I don't need to know those details. What I do know is that it is not in the nature of love to create and then abandon or annihilate. I also know, deep inside my soul, that God is love and that the identity God has given us will not be obliterated. There is a connection between who we are now and who we will be after death.

In the funeral service in the Book of Common Prayer these words are said: "Remember thy servant, [Hugh] O Lord, according to the favor which thou bearest unto thy people, and grant that, increasing in knowledge and love of thee, he may go from strength to strength, in the life of perfect service."

I believe that. Our identity, our self, our soul, goes on growing to a deeper fullness in love of God, leading us toward the kind of maturity God planned for us in the first place. For now, that is all I need to know.

Sonnet 2

How long your closet held a whiff of you,
Long after hangers hung austere and bare.
I would walk in and suddenly the true
Sharp sweet sweat scent controlled the air
And life was in that small still living breath.
Where are you? since so much of you is here,
Your unique odour quite ignoring death.
My hands reach out to touch, to hold what's dear
And vital in my longing empty arms.
But other clothes fill up the space, your space,
And scent on scent send out strange false alarms.
Now of your odour there is not a trace.
But something unexpected still breaks through
The goneness to the presentness of you.

Madeleine

Questions: 1985

Beside me, under the sheet, his shape
is blurred, his breath irregular, racing
or slowing to the stress/release
of dreams. One lung—a wing of air—
has been already clipped. The scans
show the dark shadows on his bones.

His house of cells—blue-printed
by heredity, assembled season
by season, (the grayed wood
shrinking a little at the joins
under the wash of time and storm)—
will it collapes like a barn
settling into its field?
His spirit—iridescent as a pigeon—
will it escape before mine
through a break in the roof,
homing, homing through the sky?

Luci

Snakes in the Garden:

Jealousy, tyranny, and other risks

It is not enemies who taunt me —
   I could bear that;
it is not adversaries who deal
   insolently with me —
   I could hide from them.
But it is you, my equal,
   my companion, my familiar friend,
with whom I kept pleasant company;
   we walked in the house of God
   with the throng....

My companion laid hands on a friend
   and violated a covenant with me
with speech smoother than butter,
   but with a heart set on war;
with words that were softer than oil,
   but in fact were drawn swords.

PSALM 55

To a Long Loved Love: 7

Because you're not what I would have you be
I blind myself to who, in truth, you are.
Seeking mirage where desert blooms, I mar
Your *you*. Aaah, I would like to see
Past all delusion to reality:
Then would I see God's image in your face,
His hand in yours, and in your eyes his grace.
Because I'm not what I would have me be,
I idolize Two who are not any place,
Not you, not me, and so we never touch.
Reality would burn. I do not like it much.
And yet in you, in me, I find a trace
Of love which struggles to break through
The hidden lovely truth of me, of you.

Madeleine

A Personal Story

Madeleine

Without my friends, I think I would shrivel up and die. Even so, it has not always been easy for me to have friends. As a shy, slightly lame, only child, I did not know how to reach out to other people. Perhaps my shyness seemed unfriendly. I longed for friends, but I felt left out.

One year when I was about ten, a new girl came to school in the middle of the year and for some reason reached out to me. I cared for her immediately. I thought she cared for me. We went to each other's apartments after school to do homework, to play. I was truly, deeply happy.

Then, one morning I went into school and saw her surrounded by a group of other girls, by the "popular" girls. I was out. It was as though our friendship had never existed. I had no idea what had happened. I was not prepared. It was like a deep wound which provides its own temporary anesthesia. And then the pain came.

I wanted friends. Real live friends. I loved Emily Starr and Sarah Crewe and the Little Prince. I lived largely in a world of imagination. I did not yet write well enough to love my fictional characters; they came out of wish fulfillment, though they helped to some extent. Sometimes I was happily solitary, but too often I was lonely. I longed for friends. What was wrong with me?

When I was fourteen, on our return from several years in

Europe, I was sent to a boarding school in Charleston, South Carolina, and suddenly the pattern changed. My teachers appreciated my work. The other students didn't seem to mind that I was a poor runner. When partners were chosen I wasn't the last one or the one left out. With a sudden shock I realized that I was liked! Having experienced the disappointments and hurts of being open to friendship, and being hurt and rebuffed, I was beginning to experience the joys of friendship.

Coming into friendship is only a first step. There are still risks. The day sometimes comes in a friendship when you realize you are simply hanging in there while your friend is too tangled in other concerns to be available. The time apart can be worth it, and you can learn from your absence from each other. However, sometimes the wait is in vain and you come to realize your friend is no longer there for you. Sometimes you know why. Perhaps people have been discovered who are more important, more interesting. You might wonder then whether your friendship had ever been mutual. Or, sometimes your paths have so diverged that you can't find a place to meet anymore. Sometimes you just don't know what has happened. And it hurts. I know this from personal experience, and you may well too.

But, for the most part, there are friends who are forever part of you and your journey. Those you can cry with, sharing griefs and faults. Those you can laugh with, free and joyful as small children in uninhibited mirth. Those who have proven time and again that they can be counted on. Those you can pray with on the deepest level, exposing yourselves totally to God's love. I have been richly blessed by such friends, and for each of them I daily give deep thanks.

Yes, friendship is risky. But, the risk is worth it. It is worth it to strip off your protective coating. To be vulnerable. To be known. To risk being loved.

***

The risk of love

The risk of love
is that of being
unreturned.

For if I love too deep,
too hard, too long,
and you love little,
or you love me
not at all,
then is my treasure given,
gone,
flown away lonely.

But if you give me back
love for my love
and add your own
dark fire to light my heart
then love is perfect
warm, round, augmented,
whole, endless, infinite
and it is fear that flies.

Luci

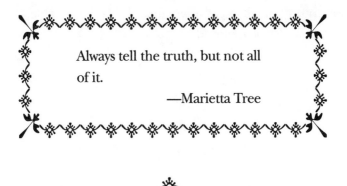

> Always tell the truth, but not all of it.
>
> —Marietta Tree

❀

Luci's Journal Entry

How many times I have been over this ground, but seeing S. today brought it all up again. What is a true friend? How can I tell a true one from a false one? Perhaps we only learn the difference by contrasting the life patterns of the one with the other. (The proof is in the pudding!) But we see them lived out in the actions of Peter and Judas.

Peter, for all his false starts, his injudicious assumptions, his rash words and actions, was wholehearted. He wore his heart on his sleeve. You knew where you stood with Peter. And he learned from his mistakes—abandonment of Jesus in an hour of need, fear of what people would think—came back from failure, and tried again.

Judas was more complicated, had a divided heart—part of it devoted to Jesus (he couldn't have been chosen by Jesus, have lived and worked with him for three years, without being profoundly influenced for good) but the other part was secretly reserved for Judas alone. Dissembling, so that his small embezzlements were hidden from the group, or rationalized ("Some of those shekels were given to the poor!"), the love of money ate at his heart, corrupting him, and in the end resulting in his subversion to greed, spurring him into the betrayal of Jesus for a few chunks of dead silver. He even betrayed his own false self, when his guilt shattered him into suicide by hanging.

Even true friends make mistakes, misjudging, forgetting, losing touch. I surely do and have and likely will. But if the heart is open, forgiveness and reconciliation wait to be found around the next corner.

My prayer: God, give me an undivided heart. "Unite my heart to fear your name" (Psalm 86:11). Untangle my mixed motives. Remove the threads of self-interest. Help me to give and receive with open hands, a Peter, maybe, but not a Judas.

Judas, Peter

because we are all betrayers, taking
silver and eating
body and blood and asking
(guilty) is it I and hearing
him say yes
it would be simple for us all
to rush out
and hang ourselves

but if we find grace
to cry and wait
after the voice of morning
has crowed in our ears
clearly enough
to break our hearts
he will be there
to ask us each again
do you love me?

Luci

Life is an endless cycle of song
a medley of extemporania
and love is a thing that can never go wrong,
and I am Marie of Romania.

—Dorothy Parker

Meeting Christ in One Another:

The earthly encounter

Salutation

Framed in light,
Mary sings through the doorway.
Elizabeth's six month joy
jumps, a palpable greeting,
a hidden first encounter
between son and Son.

And my heart turns over
when I meet Jesus
in you.

Luci

Epiphany

Unclench your fists,
Hold out your hands.
Take mine.
Let us hold each other.
Thus is his Glory
Manifest.

Madeleine

Where Do I Meet Christ?

Madeleine

In the snow and ice of a brutal winter, I struggled with my cane to climb over the frozen and slippery snow drifts that blocked the street crossings. Almost invariably, a hand would reach out for me, an arm would go about my waist, and one of the street people who rest on these street corner benches would help me across.

Christ.

Christ in clothing inadequate for the weather, smelling of unwashed body and not enough food.

Christ.

When the little Italian restaurant across the street closed down, how I missed the warm greetings of the owners and waiters, particularly Miguel. When he was there I was greeted with a kiss on each cheek, and Miguel saying: "Your garlic bread's on me."

Christ.

Then there are friends, who know, love, who just are—for me—Christs.

You are a distinct portion of the essence of God; and contain part of him in yourself. Why, then, are you ignorant of your noble birth? Why do you not consider whence you came? Why do you not remember, when you are eating, who you are who eat; and whom you feed? Do you not know that it is the Divine you feed; the Divine you exercise? You carry a God about with you, poor wretch, and know nothing of it.

—Epictetus, 50 A.D.

A *continuing conversation*

LUCI: Coming together before God, in prayer, is an integral part of our friendship—part of our daily pattern, when we're together—being together and with a sense of God's presence with us.

MADELEINE: Those prayers join our hearts and give us a way to make something whole out of our days. Early in the day with Morning Prayer we can place ourselves in God's presence as we begin our day. In the evening, at Compline, in God's loving presence we can sort out all that has happened during the day.

LUCI: Whether or not we have the Prayer Book, our friendship gives us the freedom to pray spontaneously, without inhibition, in conversation with God and each other.

MADELEINE: The fact that we can pray together doesn't necessarily mean that our faith is always constant and secure. I think I reach out for other people's prayers most when my own faith is most wobbly.

LUCI: There's an ease, too, in praying for each other over the phone. Even though my son John, and his wife Christa, are far away in South Africa, I can be joined in prayer with them over those thousands of miles, can hear the voice tones of love and concern, or relief and gratitude. And I know I can phone you, Madeleine, and say, "Tonight I don't even feel like praying. Will you pray for me? I'm feeling depressed."

MADELEINE: I know that after my San Diego accident I could not pray. I was too sick to pray, except for the Jesus Prayer. But I knew I was being prayed for, and that was enough. It's like the Russian Orthodox church services which are very, very long, and it's understood that nobody is going to be focused on what's going on all of the time. It's impossible. But *somebody* there *is* always focused, always praying, and so the focus is unbroken. I always know that when I can't pray, others can. And sometimes when they can't pray, I can. So the circle of prayer is not broken.

LUCI: Yes, and that's like what Thomas did in his time of doubt about Jesus' resurrection. He could hardly bring himself to believe that Jesus was alive with his friends again. But because he was "with the company of believers," part of the body of disciples who stayed together, he was there when Jesus showed himself to them, and gave Thomas the opportunity to test his physical reality.

MADELEINE: Yes. We can be there for each other, carrying each other along in times of need.

173

... I find a seat in the circle of others.
As our glances meet, Christ looks out from
the brown eyes, and the blue. His presence presses
lightly on us all, each, the unseen hand
moving in blessing from head to head...

... in a back row, a child makes a soft sound...

A cross unites the space, its arms embracing our
diversity, its shaft both pointing up and reaching
down. As the Word comes incarnate in us each, spoken,
broken once again, love rises in a silent incense, a unison
of silver sound, from all our hearts and throats.

Luci
from the poem,
"At the Church of the Savior, Washington, D.C.,"

Three on an Island

Madeleine

Once on the holy island of Iona, Luci, Bara and I read the Night Prayers from *A New Zealand Prayer Book* in the ruins of an old convent. The island was crowded with tourists, and we needed to get away and be alone, and the old stones of the convent were quiet and empty.

It is good to have prayer time with friends and the words of the night office are beautiful. There is plenty of space for impromptu prayers, surrounded by the beauty of the words, many from the earliest centuries of Christendom, so I was glad to be saying them in Iona, where Celtic Christianity flourished, with its tender emphasis on the earthy, the particular.

We gave thanks for the nuns of long ago who had sung the daily office, and for their souls; they had been brutally murdered for their faith, and their convent burned and vandalized. Even in those tumbled old stones we could feel ringing clear from centuries past their praise of God. United in space, in God's love, and eternal time, we prayed.

The angels of God guard us through the
night,
and quieten the powers of darkness.

The Spirit of God be our guide
to lead us to peace and to glory.

It is but lost labour that we haste to rise up
early, and so late take rest,
and eat the bread of anxiety.
For those beloved of God are given gifts
even while they sleep.

—from *A New Zealand Prayer Book*
Church of the Anglican Province
of New Zealand

The Holiness of Iona

"where two or three are gathered..."

How our Celtic blood stirred as we
navigated along the single car track
across Mull, westward between the purplish hills,
under the torn cloth of clouds, and then
over the final channel, its green-gray waves
chipping away at the hull of the ferry.
The buffet of sea-wind felt rough
as the breath of God. We could hardly wait
to settle in, to inhale
the holy island's scent of sanctity.

And it was all so lovely—the sea
between the rocks a clear bottle green over
white sand. Vivid cottage gardens
clustered beyond the jetty,
bordered with delphiniums, rank with
nasturtiums. Scores of eager day-trippers
with their back-packs and bikes crowded
the black-topped path of the Abbey;
tourists laced the air with
syllables we struggled to recognize.
The craft shops, with their local pottery
and Celtic jewelry. The gift shops, even in
the Abbey—bookmarks, scarves
like butterflies, key-rings, post-cards.

We'd expected to find Columcille,
and Patrick—the ancient saints
blessing us with a benediction
of solitude, with a peace that drops
like fading light behind the rocks.
All we sensed was...an absence. We all
missed something. We all said that we missed it—
like the wild gold of the iris blooms
whose dark summer leaves hugged
the creases of the island, their spring boldness
faded to a single wilted rag here, there.

Later, a walk together across the
close-cropped velvet and up
over the backbone of rock to a bay pebbly
as Galilee, a meal of fish
and soda-bread. An evening prayer
in the guest room, small as a cell,
showed us where to look, how to see: Our
high anticipation had detoured us
away from holiness, and when we least
expected it, there it was, God's felt presence
in our human trinity of longing.

Luci

Looking for Bread Crumbs:

Glimpses of God

And the Word became flesh and lived among us, and we have seen his glory, the glory as of a father's only son, full of grace and truth.... From his fullness we have all received, grace upon grace.

JOHN 1:14, 16 (NRSV)

Grace is everywhere. We don't own it and we cannot control it. We can only see it, receive it, and respond to it. That means to act gracefully ourselves, and the best way to do that is to thank the "author of grace" for all those who bear it, live it, and give it. And to try to go and do likewise. That is prayer.

—John B. Coburn
Grace in All Things

✳

A continuing conversation

MADELEINE: I know that some people think I'm very odd to believe in a God who is so loving. So many of them have not been taught to believe in a loving God who seeks us out, but rather an angry judge, who comes around to dispense punishment.

LUCI: Thank God you're odd! I like your kind of oddity. I think I'm rather odd, too.

MADELEINE: You're odd; you're definitely odd. Thank God. I think all of our lives and our searches have led us to allow the God of love to find us. We don't find the God of love; love finds us.

LUCI: And he doesn't always appear to us automatically, like turning on a God-faucet. Often we have to wait in patience for his timing.

MADELEINE: It's tough love, too. The answer is sometimes "No."

LUCI: Sometimes the answer is simply silence; God saying: "Learn in my absence. I'm not really far away, but I'm waiting for you to learn something you can only learn in the dark."

MADELEINE: I've also discovered that sometimes when I feel farthest from God it is I who am distanced, not God who is distant from me. I do know that God yearns for us. Yearns for us to seek. Yearns for us to come close, to stay near.

Feeding on God's crumbs

Luci

In childhood many of us listened to the story of Hansel and
Gretel, the brother and sister lost in the forest, who found
their way home by following the trail of shining stones they
had dropped behind them, one by one. In their next forest
excursion they forgot to bring stones. All they had was their
lunch bread, so they scattered behind them crumbs broken off
from their loaf. But when they turned homeward all the
crumbs had been devoured by birds, and they were hopelessly
lost. At this point in the story I would always murmur, mentally,
"But at least the hungry birds got some lunch!"

Often I feel like one of those hungry birds, pecking bread
crumbs left by other people, even fragments I've dropped
myself, and forgotten. I thank God for such provender, small
as it may seem, because it has been broken and crumbled from
Christ's own body, the eucharistic loaf of his provision, which is
made up of the coarse grain of ordinary life, and has been
baked by him into holy bread.

Perhaps that's why the symbols of bread and wine, Christ's
body and blood at the eucharistic feast, hold such profound
meaning for me. It is a time-honored exchange. At Communion I come to the altar with all my flaws and failings, my
bruises and my hungers, and that imperfect gift of myself is what
I offer to Christ—my hands open, lifted in front of me in relin-
quishment. When the priest places the broken bread on my
open palm I am receiving, in return, the gift of Christ himself—

his completeness for my inadequacy, his strength for my weakness, his love for my lack of love. When the chalice of wine is offered to me I lift my thirsty, open mouth and gulp down the symbol of Christ's life blood—a life-giving transfusion which reinvigorates my tired spirit.

Another way in which I find my way home, following the clues of bread crumbs—especially fragments of myself broken off in the past, and often forgotten, is to keep my private, reflective journal, a chronological gathering of seed ideas, theories worked through to a tentative conclusion, beginnings of poems, conversations, prayers, plans, quotes, notes—the stories that flow into my own life experience, recorded in the heat of the moment, as they happen.

The journal is my collection jar, much like the jars we children used to prepare to keep the lightning bugs we caught on the lawn in the twilight. The words in my journal blink with their own light, as I reread them. Some significant entries I've forgotten completely. Bread crumbs. Lightning bugs. Seminal insights from my own past life which feed my soul and shed light in the present moment. And in which I can often hear whispers of grace.

Sometimes I read a couple of journals straight through. A good time to do that—it takes a chunk of uninterrupted reading and concentration—is when I go camping alone for a week a couple of times each year, taking time out for my own personal retreats. That's when I can see cause-and-effect relationships, and the large patterns of God at work in my life, with greater clarity. In the pressures of daily living it's hard for me to "see the forest for the trees." But reading though an old journal is like taking a helicopter ride, high above the ground. From that elevation I can clearly see the contours of the hills and rivers, the way the trees clump, then break into a clearing of meadow grass. The whole landscape is open to view. And I need that God's-eye view of my life, not bogged down in the undergrowth of details and trivialities. I can see my own swamps of despair rising into higher ground. I can see over-arching grace and mercy. I can see how God has worked all the details of the landscape together, for my good. I can even see the bread crumbs, strewn upon the path by a loving hand.

Spiritual Direction, and Sacramental Confession

Madeleine

I'm not sure when the words "spiritual director" came into my vocabulary. Certainly during school and college I was under the "direction" of my teachers and professors, intuitively choosing those I felt were closest to understanding me realistically, and who expected the best of me. When I was working in the theater I looked up to serious theater people who understood their work as a service.

During our years of living in the country I felt an occasional unnamed loneliness. No husband, however rich and full the relationship, should be expected to serve as "spiritual director." I had many long and wonderful discussions with one of our ministers, who became one of my closest friends. In the 1950s the term "spiritual director" was not used, as far as I know, in the Congregational church—now the United Church of Christ (U.C.C.)—we belonged to. While Ray and I un-abashedly shared our problems and concerns, we did not understand ourselves to be spiritual director and directee. He was my very good and true friend, and when he left for another church I missed him sorely.

When Hugh and I and the children moved back to New York, through the help of friends we found a small and excellent school close to home. Then we looked for a church.

Unfortunately, in the 1960s many Episcopal churches still practiced "closed communion." Since I was certainly not going to any church that would not welcome Hugh at the altar rail, we tried several Congregational churches, but found them neither welcoming nor exciting. Then we discovered the Cathedral of St. John the Divine, about a mile from our apartment, in easy walking distance, and where any hungry searcher was welcome at the altar.

At the Cathedral, I quickly discovered that the Episcopal church in which I had grown up had experienced significant liturgical changes. During my early years of church-going, the service usually consisted in Morning Prayer and sermon, with the Communion Service held only on the first Sunday of the month. Now, the Communion Service was central. This immediately changed my feelings from looking at the church as reasonable, intellectual, and uninspiring, to a place of mystery and the wonder of sacrament.

Often our children's school had services at the Cathedral, and we got to know many of the nuns, and found them delightful and intelligent. Friends. I still didn't hear about spiritual direction. The nuns talked to me about confession.

Confession? Wasn't it only Roman Catholics who went to confessors, and who stood or knelt in dark little confessional boxes where they could barely see the priest, and then went over a long list of sins? As a cradle Episcopalian, I was truly surprised to be given a pamphlet with the prayer before confession and then the long list of confessable sins. It explained that, after confessing, one was absolved by the priest and given a penance, such as saying ten Hail Marys. It didn't make sense to me.

Isn't it so, however, that things have a way of converging? Evelyn Underhill has said that there is no such thing as coincidence; it is God's universe in the act of rhyming. At about this time a producer friend of my husband's asked me to read a French play about the 17th Century nun, Mariana Alcoforado, to see if he might be interested in having it translated and put into production. I read it and felt that it was poorly written and purely pornographic. I sent in my report and the producer lost interest. I didn't. I was intrigued by the possibilities of the story and did a good bit of research. Sister Mariana was not a fictional character but an historical figure. And, she had a confessor. I felt that if I wanted to try my hand at writing about Mariana, I needed to know something about confession firsthand.

Also, at that point in my life I was at an impasse in human relations; I needed to love someone I found myself unable to love, and willing myself to love was no help at all.

I knew there was weekly confession at a midtown church, so I took myself there at the appointed time. I had my list of printed confessable sins, not one of which really touched on my problem. The session was not a success, for my own soul's health, or for my understanding of Mariana.

Something, some mixed motives, made me stick at it. A month passed, with other failed attempts, before I found myself sitting in St. Martin's chapel in the Cathedral beside the priest who was to become my beloved Canon Tallis, my lifelong friend. He was formidable and I was nervous, but I explained that the list of sins did not work for me. I needed to talk about what was on my heart, what was causing pain to me and those I loved and those I could not love.

He listened. Truly listened. He did not let me off the hook. Neither did he let me wallow in false guilt. His silence forced me to be real. We met once a month for as long a session as needed. He waved no magic wands. He was my spiritual friend and my confessor. And I always left him reminded again that I was God's beloved child.

I think the concept of spiritual direction is often more accepted than sacramental confession, even in churches such as mine with a tradition of "the reconciliation of a penitent." When sacramental absolution is given, our sins are not only forgiven, they are washed away. Gone. Vanished. We are not meant to keep picking at them like an old scab but to let them go completely.

Canon Tallis and I had the kind of friendship that grew from two aspects of his priestly ministry: being my confessor and, as I later came to understand the term, my spiritual director. Together we looked for the signs of God, the glimpses of grace. Surely when someone walks with you along the path, looking for breadcrumbs, it is a magnificent manifestation of a special kind of friendship: a Trinitarian friendship, with God the apex of the triangle.

In the sacrament of reconciliation Christians can and do receive the forgiveness of God—not as a general truth or a vague promise, but personally, immediately, in actual experience. It can and does take hold of them in a living way….

The heart of God has been yearning all along for you to experience forgiveness personally, and every stage of your approach is marked by love.

—Martin L. Smith, SSJE
Reconciliation

Dear Madeleine,

I'm sitting here at my desk, just full of the sense of wonder and joy that always comes when I suddenly realize that God is at work behind the scenes, "working things together for good" for me.

You know some of the history of my searches and findings of spiritual directors. How Eugene Peterson suggested I go about this process: "Pray, and see whose name or face comes to mind." Which is how I found my first director in Chicago—the wonderful cleric who introduced me to Ignatian spiritual disciplines. But when I moved to California, the search and the prayer began over again, after an abortive encounter with a staff member at the local retreat center.

At a retreat for the women of my church, Holy Trinity Menlo Park, my prayer was answered. M.R. was our retreat leader, a young woman half my age whose quiet wisdom and creative humor I found refreshing and spiritually invigorating. After the retreat was over I asked for her business card. It read: "Retreats and Spiritual Direction." When I phoned her later and asked "Are you open to taking on new directees?" she replied, "Let's get together and talk about it."

I know from past experience how important it is to find "a good fit" in one's spiritual director. I'm not looking for a peer, or a priest, though often the function is priestly. Perhaps what I'm looking for is more like an experienced companion on the way. And in the quiet of her home, with her young baby asleep in another room, we introduced ourselves, each to the other, talking and praying and exploring our spiritual "fit."

I told her some of my conservative Christian background, and how some of those elements of faith are still very necessary for me. I have a hard time, for instance, calling God "She," or "Her," or "Mother," because though I believe that God is beyond gender, Jesus calls him Father, and having had a loving and affirming father myself, God's Fatherhood is reinforcement for me. I also believe what C. S. Lewis said, that in the presence of God the Creator, the Initiator, all of us, whether men or women, are "eternally feminine."

I told M.R. some of my past doubts and questions, my griefs and spurts of growth, and how, beneath everything else, I am a truth-seeker. She needed to know I'm not satisfied with easy answers. Platitudes make me nauseated. I don't just want to be reassured and comforted, but I need a spiritual guide who will challenge me and hold me accountable for my choices and the directions I'm finding.

When we next met, she'd provided a glass of cool water next to my chair, and before talking together we sat quietly, collecting ourselves, centering in to God in silent prayer, breathing deeply to reoxygenate our bodies and our spirits. I'm such a sacramentalist. This deep breathing speaks to me not just of physical calming, but of God's breath, his Spirit, being invited into my deepest being, a wind to scour out false assumptions and guide me into truth.

M.R. has degrees in theology and psychology, and she is aware and informed at that intellectual level. But what means the most to me is her *listening* heart. She listens to me (and remembers, with amazing clarity, the personal details that she hears from month to month) and she listens to what God is speaking into our conversation. Time and time again I find her listening, then touching the precise knot which has me bound, or putting together, and making sense out of the diverse aspects of a spiritual conundrum. She makes apt use of metaphor, which endears her to me particularly. And when I write my fears or experiences into a poem, she responds to its deepest truth without having to have it explained to her. She affirms what is healthful in me and questions anything that is spurious or superficial. Our monthly sessions are always highlights for me. I leave her with journal notes which give me much food for thought and I also note in my journal her challenges and assignments for the coming month.

Because, of course, my journal is one of the best aids in this spiritual pilgrimage, I read her my passages of intimate insights and decisions, of conflict or struggle, confident of her confidentiality. So, you can tell something very good has come into my life, a good person, one in whom I meet Jesus so powerfully. Maybe I can sum it up by saying that when I am with her, it is like being with Jesus, he is so powerfully present, and I hear his voice in her voice, see his face in hers. I write this knowing it will give you joy too.

I'll call you soon, perhaps even before you read this.

Loving you,
Luci

Sometimes we conceal our relation with God in prayer because we are afraid that others are closer than we are, that someone may be further ahead. But once we have turned and are actually seeking to confront the Other, then we will almost certainly find a need for someone to talk with. Real confrontation with love demands sharing of this experience. And in the sharing we realize that all of us, even the best, are babes in the woods.

—Morton T. Kelsey
The Other Side of Silence

Finding myself

I am leaving a trail of
crumbs
broken off from my body
to feed friends, or the birds.
Or so I have always felt
as I shoulder the branches
aside and strike deep
into the woods
where grass overgrows
the old tracks.

Ahead of me now, on
the dark ground,
abruptly shines a white thing;
it wicks like
a lamp. And another.
I hear myself humming
an old song—a round —
as I stoop and finger
my own blaze of bread
turned hard as bone.

Luci

Companions on the Way:

A foretaste of heaven

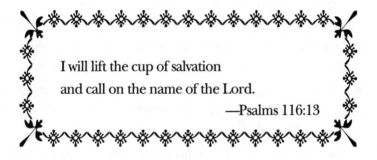

I will lift the cup of salvation
and call on the name of the Lord.

—Psalms 116:13

Madeleine

Outside the windows of my apartment an icy sleet was falling. Luci and I looked down at the street to see people struggling with umbrellas. One man slipped on the glazed sidewalk and almost fell. We looked at each other. Our plan had been to walk over to the Cathedral for the noon Eucharist.

"Madeleine, this is absurd," Luci said. "With my bad ankle and your bad knee we can't walk over there in this weather."

Reluctantly I agreed. I felt the need of the holy symbols. If I were younger I'd just have bundled up and sloshed over to the cathedral. But I'd recently had surgery. If I fell on the ice I could really be in trouble.

Luci said, "There's that really good tuna salad in the fridge. Let's have sandwiches and maybe a cup of soup and make our lunch a kind of 'sacramental meal.'

That was a grace-filled suggestion for me. All meals are sacramental, but we could make this especially so. We brought our prayer books to the small table by the big window which looked out on the increasing storm. We read the Eucharistic Prayer, and then we prayed the Prayer of Thanksgiving, and it was all a beautiful whole. No one consecrated those elements except God and us, but in the context of what we were doing we felt that they were truly consecrated. We felt no pride or self-sufficiency whatsoever, and it was deeply sacramental.

I could not have done this with somebody who did not feel as Luci and I do about the holiness of Communion. A very deep affirmation of friendship is having eucharist together. At its most basic you could say that you can't eat God together without being affected in a profound way.

As we ate our tuna sandwiches we talked about how important eating together was in the Hebrew Testament days, and still is in the Middle East today. It was understood that if you ate with someone, you could not kill that person. That was why the shaking of hands between Yasir Arafat and Shimon Peres at the peace treaty did not really assure me of peace, because the two leaders had been invited to dine in the White House and they did not accept the invitation. They would not eat together. And my heart was sad.

Luci said, "The body and blood of Christ is the supreme nourishment for the spirit. Without it we are really impoverished. Remember what Gerard Manley Hopkins said, 'To go to Communion worthily gives God great glory, but to take food in thankfulness and temperance gives him glory, too.' There are so many Christian denominations that seldom practice Communion, and maybe that's one of the reasons the Christian church as a whole is deprived of this whole sacramental view of life which you and I find so meaningful."

I agree. It binds us together in a way nothing else can. I do find a hunger for the sacramental in people who have had little experience of it. Several of my United Church of Christ friends are now approaching the communion service in a much more sacramental way than they used to. Charlie Russ, the retired minister who was so close to Hugh and me during Hugh's illness, celebrated communion in our village church in a way that was so humbly full of the mystery of the Word made flesh that I felt right at home.

There's often a double helix in the Protestant tradition, a

hunger for sacrament, and a need for explanation that expresses itself in good works—necessary good works but without the mystery of knowing that our good works are not ours.

The next day was cold but clear, so after our morning's work Luci and I headed for the Cathedral. Our first stop was the Library, where I have my desk. There was nobody in the library at the moment. We continued our conversation as we straightened up a bit and shelved books, including a recent one on the importance of grounding social action in a life of prayer. A prayer life prepares you for something far beyond any notions of simply being "right-minded," or "politically correct."

Luci said, "When Jesus was reprimanded for eating with his politically incorrect friends, he reminded the religious leaders that he had come for those who are sick, not those who are well, and that what he wants is mercy, not sacrifice. Mercy stands for loving and self-giving. Sacrifice stands for the politically correct system of ceremonial laws, prohibitions, and sacrificial offerings."

We agreed that it is hilarious for Christians to be politically correct when we follow a Man who was so politically incorrect that he got crucified for it. We wondered if you can feel politically correct without having your heart in it. You don't have to hurt for the people you are simply being politically correct about.

"My son John feels that the personal involvement, feeling the hurt with hurting people, counts so much. I was once put to shame by him about that," Luci said. "I met him briefly in Washington, D.C., and suggested that I take him out to dinner, to some quiet place where we could talk and catch up. He said to me, 'Mother, if I meet a needy person who asks me for money, well, I won't give money but I will ask him or her out for dinner. Are you willing to go along with me on that?' I knew that would really be a sacrifice to give up my time with him but I respected John's suggestion."

There was a long silence. Luci and I do not always agree, and this was one of those times. I said "I'm having real trouble with this. John doesn't see you that often. He sees panhandlers every day. I'm asked for money half a dozen times when I walk down the street. Sometimes I offer food from one of the many little eateries in my block. It is a hard call. One friend of mine who really struggles to make ends meet asks for the name of the person and says she will pray for that person by name."

Luci continued, "John feels that you need to enter the life of the person who is asking to experience a loving under-standing. It's much easier to give a dollar. Taking a meal together demands more."

I was still unhappy, still unconvinced. Through a deep sigh I said, "Luci, we cannot connect with everybody's need. If I eat a hamburger with a panhandler, how much connecting am I really doing? We'll probably never meet again. I do try to con-nect in prayer as much as possible. But that one special evening with you and John, well, I still feel that the important thing was for you to have dinner with your son, for him to have dinner with his mother."

Of course, all our conversation is not on this intense level. But we were constantly thinking about this book on friendship we were struggling to write, and everything we talked about seemed to touch on it.

It was time for the Eucharist and we made our way across the close to the Cathedral and St. Martin's chapel. We nodded and smiled at several of the regular communicants as we went to our seats. It is a greeting quite different from the usual social interchange. We took our places and crossed ourselves ("Don't be afraid of making the sign of the cross," an Anglican monk once told me. "All it means is: God be in my thoughts, in my heart, in my left hand, in my right hand, all through this day.") and prepared once again to share this holy meal together, to rejoice in saying "thank you" to God for being with us in Eucharist—which in Greek means *thank you.*

Friendship with God used to mean friendship with the God of one small planet. Now, it means friendship with the God of the galaxies, more galaxies than we can count, a God whose creativity is so enormous it is beyond our comprehension. Maybe that's why the Lord's Table is so important to me. It is God reminding me that divine love is always personal and that God shows us total intimacy in the incarnation and the Eucharist.

The familiar prayers were said, the bread was broken and given. *"The Body of Christ, the bread of heaven. The Blood of Christ, the cup of salvation."*

I don't think we can connect single-handedly with the needs of everyone, but the body of Christ is not single-handed, and many can do what one cannot. We do know this: God's Son was sent for everyone, the whole broken and needy world. The bread is broken for all of us. Our companionship in Christ strengthens us to go out to the world, and to those who do not come to the altar. And, we go knowing that we will be strengthened to respond to God's people and shown the way.

Luci and I returned from the communion rail and took our seats, fed and deeply grateful. With our companions in the chapel we said the familiar words of the closing prayer.

Eternal God, heavenly Father, you have graciously accepted us as living members of your Son our Savior Jesus Christ, and you have fed us with spiritual food in the Sacrament of his Body and Blood. Send us now into the world in peace, and grant us strength and courage to love and serve you with gladness and singleness of heart; through Christ our Lord. Amen.

We left and made our way home, carrying within us the body of Christ.

Spring: St. Martin's Chapel

Both of us kneel, then wait
on the church chairs—square, chocolate brown —
knowing that soon the black priest

will hurry in, wearing his lateness like
the wrong robe. In the pregnant emptiness
before communion, that crack between worlds,

we listen inward, feet tight on the cold slate,
wanting to hear Christ tell us *Feed on me.*
Our hearts shiver, hidden. Nothing visible moves.

Outside a drizzle starts; drops spit on the sill.
The window bird flies motionless in
a cobalt sky of skillful glass.

But beyond the frame, plucking the eye
like a message from Outside, a minor shadow
tilts and swoops in light rain,

wings telling us to fly wide, loose
and nervy as pigeons who may peck crumbs from
any picnic table, or gnats right out of the air.

Luci

A continuing conversation

LUCI: I can test my ideas with you. I can argue with you, and the dialogue helps me understand what I'm feeling and whether or not it's valid.

MADELEINE: Me, too, which is at the center of our understanding of being together on this life journey—following Christ. Sometimes I'm with people who are "bibliolaters." They worship the Bible, but they don't necessarily read it, at least not the tough parts. The Bible is full of paradoxes and contradictions. You can prove almost anything you want from the Bible.

LUCI: Yes, when you take what you want out of context.

MADELEINE: Jesus was the Word of God, with a capital W. The word of God, with a little w, is true, but not necessarily literally factual, and that upsets a lot of people, the confusion of fact and truth. But you know how I feel about that, having so recently edited *The Rock which is Higher*, which expresses my thoughts about story as truth.

LUCI: Oh yes, indeed I do. It was fun, all of it. We had some good arguments, and some good resolutions.

MADELEINE: And, as always, a few things left to be questioned. When a child says, "Tell me a story, tell me a story!" what the child is asking for is truth and affirmation: *Yes, you matter. Yes, life is worth living.* The child knows that story is true, so children love stories, stories telling the truth about *Why am I alive? What is life about? What is my meaning? Is there a God? Does anybody care?*

LUCI: Questions like that go way beyond fact to truth.

MADELEINE: You can't put what happens at the Eucharist in terms of fact.

LUCI: It's love in action. It's *true*. It's always been a surprise to me that the true believers are very few and far between, the ones like David with a true heart towards God, the faithful remnant.

MADELEINE: It's also baffling and sad that some of the people who consider themselves to be true believers...

LUCI: ... are often the most un-Christlike.

MADELEINE: The most judgmental. The most everything Jesus told us not to be. People with no doubts, who repress doubts. And so the unknowable gets limited and squashed into the knowable.

LUCI: I've often wondered whether such Christians look at the apostle Paul as their leader and example rather than Jesus.

MADELEINE: That was my mother's theory, that Paul did great damage. I get annoyed that sometimes Paul is so marvelous and then he says something terrible! A lot of anti-Semitism comes from Paul, despite his own Jewishness.

LUCI: But Paul was human, too.

MADELEINE: If Paul had come up before a search committee looking for a new rector for their church, he wouldn't have made it past the first interview. And I sometimes wonder: whose qualifications are we looking for?

LUCI: Qualifications? I suppose we have to outline qualifications, or jobs wouldn't be done right.

MADELEINE: (Laughing.) I wouldn't want my wonderful butcher to take out my appendix, though he might be better than my dentist. It's a paradox, because the scriptural protagonists were all unqualified to do what they did. It gives us heart as we bumble along.

Gifts of Companionship

Madeleine

Perhaps Luci and I would talk less intensely, more light-heartedly (and perhaps less pompously) if we saw each other more often. Though we are in close touch, it is not the same as being together, every day, able to discuss not only what is going on in our lives and in the world, but our struggle to express in this book the meaning of friendship.

The phone has often been our prayer chain, as we've called to ask for prayers for each other, our children, our friends. There is no such thing as a full family life without crisis, and in the past few weeks I'd had to call for prayers for the serious illness of my son, now recovering, and for the deep hurt given one of my daughters. Luci has called with some of her own painful requests, and the fact that we are able to do this, almost without thinking, as a spontaneous reaction, is sacramental evidence that we are companions together on the way.

And there is much about which to pray: we live in a brutal world. Luci reminded me that it was brutal in Jesus' time, and I suppose it has always been brutal. One story is that the great flood was caused by God's tears; God was so grieved by the pain and wickedness in this planet which was created with so much love and joy that the Creator wept for forty days and forty nights.

God had cause again to weep while his Son walked the earth. During his public ministry, even the disciples didn't understand Jesus. He told them the truth, called himself a servant, talked about giving up power, and his disciples were constantly seeking for power and more power, even at the Last Supper. Perhaps that was why Jesus had such close friendships with Mary of Magdala, with Mary and Martha of Bethany, because women in his day were powerless, and were therefore more capable of understanding what he was talking about.

Recently I read an excellent novel in which a scrap of papyrus was found which was part of a letter written by Mary of Magdala, indicating that she was one of the apostles. The novel was set around the turn of the eighteenth century, and the disclosure of this potent scrap of paper would have turned the church upside down. The patriarchy which dominated the Western world would have been far more scandalized than they were by any of Darwin's discoveries. A woman an apostle! Never!

We see it differently now, at least a lot of us do, and the idea that the Mary who was the first person to whom Jesus revealed himself after the Resurrection was also one of his apostles seems quite possible, even likely. Jesus relieved her of seven demons, and surely she loved him with her whole heart. True love, pure love; not all love is genital. And if Mary loved him in all ways, that statement is hardly surprising or shocking.

Many of Jesus' parables, if we are willing not to take them literally, are telling the truth about ourselves that we really don't want to hear. They point out our hardness of heart, our smugness, our unwillingness to see ourselves as we truly are. It's a lot easier to take the parables literally than to understand that Jesus was trying to tell us something important about ourselves. Are we ungenerously resenting the return of the prodigal son? The payment of those who worked for an hour being the same as those who worked in the heat of the day? Do we want to be considered important, rather than know ourselves unworthy, like the Levite at the temple?

One of the important things about friendship is that we allow the friends of our heart to see us, not as we would like to be (none of us is what we'd like to be), but as we really are, with our weaknesses, our faults and flaws. Our view of our friends must be devoid of idolatry, which is a temptation. I've fallen into it often enough, wanting the other person to be all-wise, all-healing, all-knowing—in other words, wanting the idol to be God. But idols are idols, and never God. The human Jesus had to face all these false expectations, people wanting him to be nothing but divine, or perhaps not so much divine as magic.

A gift we are given by our companions along the way is that we can ask questions that some people might consider radical. We know that even if we may be considered momentarily shocking, or off course, our friends won't judge us harshly.

My dictionary says: *heterodox: contrary to or different from some acknowledged standard, as the Bible, a creed, etc.* Does that make me heterodox, then? For instance, I believe that God created the universe in divine time, not in human time, six days Greenwich mean time or Eastern Daylight time. Doesn't Scripture remind us frequently that God's time and ours are entirely different?

Do I believe that God sometimes reveals truth through story, rather than fact? It is more important to me to understand that God is radically forgiving than that Jonah was in the belly of an actual fish. Jonah is a wonderful story of our hard-heartedness and God's loving forgiveness.

I don't think we should ever be afraid to ask God our deepest questions because we're afraid of criticism or misunderstanding. If we can kneel at the communion rail and still ask our question, then we can trust it. And, as we find friends with whom we can share our fears, our inadequacies and struggles, our questions and confusions about our faith, then, then we will know that we have found companions along the way.

from **The Partaking**

...Often we taste the
granular body of wheat
(Think of the Grain that died!)
and swallow together
the grape's warm, bitter blood
(Remember First Fruit!)
knowing ourselves a part of you
as you took part of us,
flowed in our kind of veins,
quickened cells like ours into
a human subdividing.
Now you are multiplied —
we are your fingers and your feet,
your tender heart,
we are your broken side.

Take now, and crumble small,
and cast us on the world's waters,
your contemporary shewbread.
Feed us
to more than five thousand
women and men
and in our daily flood of living
pour yourself out again.

Luci

Luci's Journal Entry

As Madeleine and Bara and I have been working on the finishing touches of this book at Crosswicks Cottage, in Connecticut, we have been surrounded by the green folds of the Litchfield Hills. Between sessions at the computer we've made excursions to buy corn at the local farm stand, or to go to the Congregational church on Sunday, or simply to buy groceries, or take mail to the post office, driving along the winding country roads.

Very often our companion along the way, following the turns in the road as we drove, was a hand-built, low stone wall of the kind common in New England, erected as much to get the stones out of the fields as to keep the cattle from straying. It struck me today that a wall like this is a metaphor of friendship. There's some time-consuming skill involved in putting it together without cement or mortar of any kind. There's nothing artificial binding the individual pieces of rock together; they stay in place simply because they fit, the convexity of one stone nestled in the concavity of its neighbor. Even the gritty texture of the granite stones has value, preventing them from slipping apart, keeping their surfaces in touch.

When well built, these walls last for generations. They are not only useful, they are ornamental, an integral part of the landscape. Like the stones in the wall, we see the skillful hand of God at work, using even our rough, gritty surfaces, fitting us together in love, in friendship—companions along the way.

Epilogue

When we come to the end of something, it is a while before we realize that something else is beginning. Doors close, and doors open. It is hello and good-bye, and good-byes are always poignant. They are easiest when something permanent is left behind. We've come to such a good-bye. We say good-bye to this book in the middle of the beautiful stability of a long friendship that has grown and developed over many years and will, we believe, continue to do so.

Yesterday Bara came to the Cottage with the complete manuscript of *Friends for the Journey,* and we spent the day going over it. It was a glorious end-of-summer day, and we sat at the table working, accompanied by the loud sounds of sawing and hammering as the two young carpenters worked on the roof of the screened porch. The sounds of their work and laughter were, somehow, part of our own work. I looked at what Bara had done in editing and shaping this book and I was awed and delighted. We were just about to call Luci when the telephone rang and it was Luci, calling us, joining us in the Cottage by phone all the way from San Francisco.

Luci and I had just been together on this past weekend when she and John flew across the continent to New York for my granddaughter Charlotte's wedding in a Greek Orthodox church. Some of the marriage ceremony traditions I would love to see in my own church, and the loveliest thing of all was the absolute radiance in Charlotte's face. After the ceremony there was a dinner reception at the Episcopal Cathedral, with a Greek band and Greek line dancing. When I finally said good-bye to Luci and John (and that evening was surely a prime example of a hello and good-bye, an ending and a beginning) I said, "We'll talk soon. The book is almost done, isn't it?"

And I felt a certain wistfulness. This project had ensured many visits back and forth, and has deepened our intimacy, which was already deep. This deepening will continue as we keep up the habit of frequent phone calls, of praying together, going to the altar together, sharing our questions, our griefs, our joys.

But the book is finished.

Last night Bara and I went out on the terrace to look at the sky, which was crystal clear. The moon was not yet up, so the stars were brilliant, and we could see the great river of the Milky Way as it streamed across the sky. We were part of that glory, as friendship is another expression of the wonder of creation, of our tiny human part in it. And yet we know that tiny and great are the same in the eyes of the Creator, and that, too, is the wonder of stability in the midst of all the changes of life. We may not always hear the galaxies singing as they dance their great circular dance, but we echo their dance in our own ways. We echoed it in the line dancing at Charlotte and John's wedding reception, and Bara and I echoed it again, as we came into the house to read Compline and decided to sing the psalms for the evening—our own melodies.

Good-bye, little book. You have blessed us. May you give your blessing to those who read what we have written.

Madeleine

Amen. Amen.

Luci